ENDORSEMENTS

"COMPELLING is far too mild a word to describe the impact of this document. It is God's call come alive in a woman who dared listen. "Somebody's calling my name" is an old spiritual that forecasts her experience. A real faith-based adventure that is rooted in love is launched! Faith without love cannot explode in such action. 1 Corinthians 13.1-3. HEART for Africa is so appropriate—from the heart of God to the heart and soul of Janine to hearts that will listen all over the world."

—Dr. Joseph E. Lowery
Co-Founder and President Emeritus Southern Christian Leadership Conference, Joseph E Lowery Institute for Justice and Human Rights at Clark Atlanta University

---

"Janine seems to ask the question once asked by the prophet Elisha; "Is it well with you?" Janine's heart cry seems to say; "NO, it is not well with me." I believe you will hear a deep cry and heart beat for the poor through the pages of this book. My prayer is that you read through this book and respond to this same question of Elisha: "Is it well with you?" So fasten your seat belt and be blessed by this book!"

—Stephen Lungu
CEO and International Team Leader of African Enterprise

"It's a unique journey of the heart, and it's one our long-time friend Janine Maxwell and her family have been on for the last few years. From the fast-paced, daily-dollar grind of a successful international business to the heart-wrenching hopelessness in the eyes of a dying African orphan, this book will inspire you to take a deep, fresh look at what God considers truly valuable."

—Ron & Ann Mainse
Hosts of 100 Huntley Street Television

"I have been to the AIDS orphanages in the worst slums of Africa. I'm sure hell is worse, but not by much. The difference is that hell is separation from God and yet, God is in Africa giving hope to the hopeless. You cannot see this and do nothing. The Spirit of the Lord within you will not allow it. It's not okay with me either."

—Jeff Foxworthy, Comedian

"For most of us the ills of far away Africa are unfathomable. Wars, pestilence, and disease seem to keep the Dark Continent dark. Without real, human connections, Africa tends to remain a hopeless abstraction. Janine Maxwell illuminates the darkness, and brings hope in reminding us of our human connections and responsibilities. She puts faces on the suffering, changing the abstract to the tangible. She forces us to say; 'No! It's NOT okay with me!'"

—Captain Gerald Coffee, US Navy (Ret.)
Seven year Vietnam P.O.W. Author of "Beyond Survival," speaks worldwide sharing a message of faith and the invincibility of the human spirit.

"Reading Janine Maxwell's book during the time that my own daughter is working with the orphans of AIDS victims in an African medical clinic has definitely impacted my life. This book will touch you to the core of your soul and cause you to say, "It's not okay with me!" God bless Janine Maxwell for shining another light on the immense problems that are occurring in Africa. May God cause each of us to ask "What can I do to help?"

—C. David Rhodes, III, Headmaster,
King's Ridge Christian School, Alpharetta, GA

"This up-close look at the life of Janine and Ian will challenge everyday business people to consider how God might use their business skills to tackle some of the big giants in society. Beyond this, it will stir your heart with compassion for real kids with names and faces whom God used to give Janine a heart shaped like Africa. I recommend the book, and I commend the love from which it springs."

—Brett Johnson, Founder, equip. President, The Institute for Innovation, Integration & Impact, Inc. Author of Convergence, I-Operations: How to transform business using the Internet, and LEMON Leadership.

"I went on a Heart for Africa trip hoping to change lives and the first life to be changed was my own. God wants to use us to be His hands and feet in Africa. Go and be transformed."

—Lara Liptak, Heart for Africa Volunteer, Malawi 2006

IT'S NOT OKAY WITH ME

IT'S
NOT OKAY
WITH ME

by
JANINE MAXWELL

WINEPRESS **WP** PUBLISHING

WinePress Publishing (PO Box 428, Enumclaw, WA 98022) functions only as book publisher. As such, the ultimate design, content, editorial accuracy, and views expressed or implied in this work are those of the author.

Unless otherwise noted, all Scriptures are taken from the Holy Bible, Today's New International® Version TNIV©. Copyright 2001, 2005 by International Bible Society®. Used by permission of International Bible Society®. All rights reserved worldwide.

Scripture references marked MSG are taken from The Message Bible © 1993 by Eugene N. Peterson, NavPress, POB 35001, Colorado Springs, CO 80935, 4th printing in USA 1994. Published in association with the literary agency—Aline Comm. POB 49068, Colorado Springs, CO 80949. Used by permission.

"Here with Me" by Dan Muckala/Brad Russell/Pete Kipley/ Bart Millard/Nathan Cochran/Mike Scheuchzer/Jim Bryson/ Robby Shaffer/Barry Graul © 2004 Simpleville Music (ASCAP) admin. by Simpleville Music, Inc./Wet As A Fish Music (ASCAP) admin. by Simpleville Music, Inc. Used with permission.

"Voice of Truth" by Mark Hall/Steven Curtis Chapman, © 2003 Club Zoo Music/Peach Hll Songs 2/Sparrow Songs/SWECS. All Rights Reserved. Used by Permission.

ISBN 1-57921-885-7
Library of Congress Catalog Card Number: 2006937195

Printed in Colombia.

TABLE OF CONTENTS

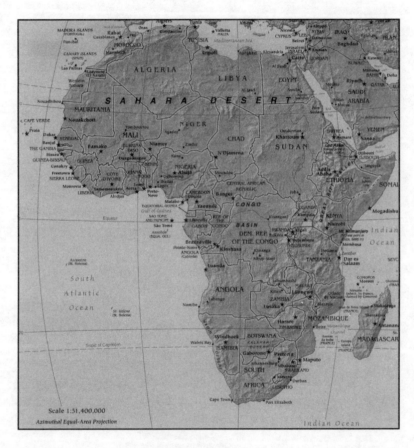

Map of Africa

INTRODUCTION

The book you are about to read is my personal journey from riches to rags, success to significance, or as my girlfriend said about me, "Marketing chick to African Chief in five agonizing years." I did not want to write this book. I did not want to tell you about my business successes and failures, my fears, my doubts, my depression or my disobedience. Frankly, I didn't think it was any of your business. But I swallowed my pride, was obedient, and wrote it. And somehow it got into your hands, so now it becomes your business.

I thought I would always own my successful marketing company, always be making money, and always be designing creative campaigns. But now I am a missionary, of sorts, and designing a new kind of campaign. You are about to read the kick-off to that campaign. I am committed to telling the world the truth about what is happening to the children of Africa and trying to get people to do something. (Hopefully, this book might help to reach the goal a bit quicker). I want everyone to look into the eyes of an African child and see the hope that I do. I want everyone who says, "It's not okay with me either," to act! To do something to make a difference. It could be as simple as baking cookies or having an annual garage sale, or as big as recruiting your small group to go to Africa with you and help out for a week or two.

The stories you are about to read are true, I have seen them with my own eyes, but I have changed a few of the names and some details to protect the people whose stories I tell.

Although the book is my story, it is really a witness to how God is calling ordinary everyday people to step up to the plate and make a difference in the world. I always thought that it was priests and pastors and reverends who were supposed to be doing God's work. But apparently I was wrong. There are far more of us "ordinary types" than there are religious leaders. Each of us has the power to change the world. Imagine the transformation that could occur if we could put our pride aside and united together. Just imagine.

Thank you for deciding to join me on this journey. Get ready for a wild ride.

From my heart to yours,
Janine

Chapter One

9/11—
THE DAY THAT CHANGED THE WORLD

The policeman outside our hotel window raised his gun and fired it into the air while yelling, "Run. Get out of the building. There is a bomb in Grand Central Station." Our hotel was directly above Grand Central Station.

We grabbed our purses and briefcases, and we ran toward the door of the hotel with hundreds of other panicked people. I suddenly realized I had forgotten my cell phone plug that had been charging my phone. I ran back to get it, thinking, *What would we do without cell phones? No one would know where we are. We would die alone and no one would find us if we couldn't call them and let them know what was happening . . .*

My friend Irene was very angry that I was running away from our exit. She screamed, "Janine, get out of the building." I grabbed the plug and pushed my way through the crowd to the revolving door. I was out. Now what? Where do we go? What is happening? The crowd was being pushed by police cars driving east on 42nd Street, sirens blaring, voices telling us to, "Move it." Everyone was trying to be calm, but there was fear in every face, except for the faces who had not heard the morning news.

Several people looked at us with wide open eyes—eyes that seemed somehow innocent, untarnished, unknowing, and unafraid—and all of this was happening in New York City. Imagine! These people left for work early that morning. Rode the train, got off, grabbed a coffee, and were making their way to the office. Some of them had opened up stores and were busy stocking shelves, selling magazines, and serving java and did not have a television or radio nearby. They must have thought us all mad as we ran past them in complete fear and unknowing. These people had not yet heard the news that two jetliners had been intentionally flown into the World Trade Center towers.

Earlier we had seen the second plane hit from the windows of my hotel room. My associates and I didn't want to stay up high in our rooms as we didn't know what building might be hit next, but we did want to be fully appraised of what was happening. We decided to go to the lobby bar on the main floor. It had not yet opened for lunch. It was only 9:15 A.M. We found a bartender preparing the coffee and putting out glasses, and kindly asked him to turn on CNN. He did. He didn't ask why and, we didn't tell him. We sat and watched.

Both planes had hit the towers and the buildings were now towering infernos. In a short time they would both collapse. We saw a report on the news that a car bomb had just blown up the Capitol building in Washington, D.C. (The report later turned out to be false.) The local NYC News ONE showed live footage of the burning structures and as we watched this live television report we witnessed terrified people jump from the buildings. We saw them jump and scream and panic and splat on the ground, on buses, and through glass roofs. This footage was not shown nationally. It was not part of the repeated footage that the world watched over and over, but I have seen it again and again and again in my own mind's eye. An endless loop tape. Hundreds of people reportedly jumped to their deaths that day. Then the news came of a plane hitting the Pentagon. And finally, we heard of a plane crashing in a field somewhere.

Over in the restaurant, tables were filled with people still calmly having breakfast meetings, discussing the critical issues of the day, and how they were going to solve them, buy them, or avoid them. They still did not know what was happening. The world had just changed forever and these people were innocently enjoying their Eggs Benedict.

Planes were dropping from the sky, and I knew instinctively that it would never end. The planes would just keep falling. No, not falling. They were being deliberately flown into tall buildings, small homes, cities, and towns all over America. America was at war. America was under attack, and I was smack dab in the middle of it.

I never came to the city in September. I live in Canada. I usually come in February for the International Toy Fair and in June for the International Licensing Show, but never in September. So what am I doing here? Oh right, the Marketing to Kids conference. But who cares about sugar cereal and kid's trends? The world is coming to an end. My world is coming to an end today. I will never see home again. I will never see my husband again. I will never see my two beautiful children, Spencer and Chloe (aged seven and five) again.

My friend and business colleague, Irene, sat at the bar staring at the three televisions that were on. The bar was filling up as the news spread. She was silent. Then she spoke as if in a trance she said, "No one will know that I am gone."

I didn't know what she meant, so I asked her, "What are you talking about?"

She repeated herself saying, "No one will know that I am gone."

As a single woman, Irene was suddenly distraught and feeling very alone.

Again I asked her what she meant and she said, "I have no husband, no children. No one will miss me. I will not leave a hole behind when I am gone."

I froze. I couldn't breathe. I held onto the bar for support. Ian, my wonderful husband of ten years was on an American

Airlines flight to Chicago from Toronto. How could I have not thought of that at the beginning? Is his plane on fire? Is it in a million pieces? Weren't the planes that were crashing and burning American Airlines planes?

America was under attack and both of us, even though we were Canadians, were under attack as well. I felt trapped. The US/Canada border was being closed. My children knew we were in America, specifically New York City. What would they think? The world began to spin. Both Ian and I were going to die. Who will raise my children? I am an only child. My parents are ailing. Ian's family lives miles away. Who will tell our children that we are dead? Who will comfort them at night? Who will pick them up from school? Who will tell them everything will be okay because it won't be okay. Who would tell them that lie?

> America was under attack and both of us, even though we were Canadians, were under attack as well.

I tried to call our office right away, but the cell lines were jammed. There were two other people in New York with Irene and me. Ray and Amanda were guests of ours at the conference. They both worked in the marketing department at Kellogg Canada, our largest account. ONYX Marketing Group, my company of thirteen years, had the exclusive Agency of Record contract with Kellogg Canada and so invited these two young marketers to New York to see what was hot and what was not for kids.

When gunshots were fired outside the hotel lobby window and we were told to run, we immediately ran the first ten blocks without stopping to rest—me in my new Adrienne Vittadini leather sling-back shoes that I had bought just the day before. Everyone was on the move like thousands of animals being herded up the street. We planned to go uptown to the bridge in Queens and cross over to Long Island. Would we ever be safe? We had no access to information. Our phones didn't work. There was no information to be had. There were very few cars on the street, just lines of people. The higher up we got on Manhattan Island, the slower the people walked and the more hopeless they looked. It seemed for each ten blocks we traveled, the look on people's faces changed from fear, to disbelief to, hopelessness.

There were no cars. Where were the cars? We stopped to regroup. Panic tried to force its way into our thinking, but we couldn't allow that to happen, not yet. We had to stay focused on the task at hand. We needed to get to a safe place. But where?

A man walked ahead of us carrying his laptop bag on his shoulder. He was covered in white dust from head to toe from the collapse of the towers. He appeared not to notice anything or anyone around him.

When we arrived at the bridge in Queens we saw thousands of people trying to cross and we got scared. We weren't going on that bridge. We were sure that it would be the next target. We were afraid it would collapse, and we would die in the river. Just then we began to hear fighter planes flying overhead. Were they "ours" or "theirs"? We quickly continued past the bridge for another ten blocks where we found a bar with few people in it. We ran inside to watch CNN to see if we were in new danger. The US Navy had been released to surround Manhattan. The question still remained: Were we safe? We plugged in the phone hoping our lifeline to the outside world would work. The next five hours were a blur. No calls could come in, but we could call out from time to time. We sat quietly and thought our own thoughts. For hours.

During this period Ian was sitting on an airplane in Chicago for five hours, going crazy. His flight had landed just before 9:00 A.M. and they would not let anyone off. He knew I was in New York. He knew of the towers being destroyed, but he couldn't reach me by phone. I could not receive any incoming calls. There were no rental cars available in Chicago by the time he got off the plane. He would have to go home by train, if he could get a ticket. The Canadian borders were closed by this point so Ian decided to go the hotel room that had been reserved for him and wait (again for hours) to hear from me. My parents came to the house to be with the children and also sat waiting to hear.

Finally, I was able to get a call through to Kellogg Canada. Immediately, they came to our rescue. We spoke with the Vice-President of Marketing, who said that Kellogg was taking responsibility for all four of us as if we were Kellogg employees. They had set up a crisis center in their offices. They would not rest until we were safely home. They worked tirelessly for hours trying to find us hotel rooms, with no luck. They worked on getting a car or train or anything to get us out. There were none.

Bridges and tunnels in and out of New York City were closed. At one point Kellogg found a friend of a friend who was a vice-president of a large advertising agency in NYC. Mary had a place on the upper west side and they were sure she would welcome us, but they had trouble contacting her. I called Mary and immediately got through to her husband. After introducing myself and explaining who we were, her husband invited us to come over. He informed us that Mary had just gone out, but would be back soon. I told him I would call back within two hours after we determined how we would get there and when we would arrive. He assured me that he would be there all day.

We continued to look for an option that would get us out of the city. Even though we were not hopeful of finding transportation, we knew that at least we had somewhere to land that was north of where we were. We called everyone we knew in the area, leaving messages everywhere we could.

Hours passed and we began to unravel. We didn't have a plan. We were tired and hungry. It would be dark soon. We had nowhere else to turn. When we talked again to the Kellogg folks, they could hear it in our voices. They told us to go to Mary's apartment and rest. The next day we needed to try to get ourselves out of Manhattan to Newark, New Jersey, as they were sending a car to pick us up there. Imagine, someone coming to get us. That was music to our ears. We cried.

At last we decided to give up on the plan of getting out of the city that day and opted to go to Mary's apartment. When I called back to say that we were on our way, Mary answered the phone. I explained, with as much cheer as I could muster, who I was. She was strangely quiet. When I finished, I asked if her husband had mentioned that I had called. She confirmed he had, but raised her concern about where we would sleep since they only had a one bedroom apartment. She felt they couldn't possibly accommodate our entire group for the night.

I was stunned. I started to laugh nervously and told her we had nowhere else to go. She said she was sorry and stated she was on call in case anyone from her building downtown might need a place to stay. They *might* call her. It was 5:00 P.M.

Even though her comment made no sense, we were desperate, so I pressed. I asked if she had any suggestions where we could go to sleep. She apologized but said she had no ideas but for us. We should call her back in an hour and she might be able to think of something. I ended the frustrating conversation, thanking her for her "help" but felt sick inside. My friends gave me a stunned look. We all laughed in disbelief and then our laughter turned to tears. We continued to unravel. We were tired, in shock, sad, and so very scared.

A car stopped on the corner and we quickly asked the driver if he could take us to New Jersey, but his car was full. He did tell us that there was a car rental place up the street. When I heard this I ran, desperately hoping to find us a way out of New York.

Even though it was after 5:00 P.M., we got the very last car, but only if I promised to bring it back to that office in New York. I lied. They rented me the car, and we were mobile.

We called Kellogg to tell them the good news that we had a rental car and they gave us even better news. They had found another place for us to stay. These were friends of a friend of a friend of the President of Kellogg Canada. But to us they were angels.

> We drove to the opposite side of Manhattan and arrived at their door like drowning dogs pulled from a river.

We drove to the opposite side of Manhattan and arrived at their door like drowning dogs pulled from a river. I was still in my high heels and my dress. My makeup was gone due to the many tears I had cried. My face was filled with exhaustion. But we had arrived and we were welcomed. Mike and Jennifer had just moved into this one bedroom flat and had not yet unpacked. There were boxes piled high, but we didn't care. It looked like a palace.

Now ladies, you are likely wondering how my feet were doing, running in brand new leather sling-backs for dozens of blocks, with no panty hose on in an 80-plus degrees New York City day. Well, let me tell you, I didn't have a single blister. In fact, once I returned to Canada, I sent a letter to the President of Adrienne Vittadini. I told him my story (small in comparison to everyone else's, but nonetheless a good shoe story for a shoe guy) and thanked him and his company for making great shoes. Ten days later I received a letter from him saying that their offices were, in fact, in downtown Manhattan, and they had suffered as everyone else had. However, my letter had provided a glimmer of hope to a company that was hurting. He went on to say that he had sent my letter to their offices all over the world to encourage the company to continue on. He then asked me an interesting question, "What size are your feet, Mrs. Maxwell? We would like to send you more shoes!" Yep, can you believe it? Two weeks later I got a brand new pair of sizzling Jones New York pumps.

Once we got settled into Mike's and Jennifer's apartment, we all sat and watched the news together. Mike's roommate from college was missing, and he spoke regularly on the phone with friends and family about others who were missing or dead, while shielding us from his pain. He knew that we were at the breaking point and didn't want to add to our burden.

Finally, I was able to reach Ian. I cried. He cried. We cried together. He was safe and sound in Chicago and was so happy to hear my voice.

> Finally, I was able to reach Ian. I cried. He cried. We cried together.

We spoke briefly and filled each other in on our "best laid plans" for the next day. He would get on a fifteen-hour Amtrak train ride back to Toronto. I would head to Newark, where we'd be picked up by our Kellogg saviors. Within twenty-four hours we should each be much closer to the Canadian border. We told each other "I love you" and hung up.

I called the kids and my parents. Mom and Dad had taken the kids horseback riding where they could not see newspapers or television. Spencer was old enough to know that I was in New York and that Daddy was in America. He would quickly put the pieces together if he had them.

It was getting late at this point so the four of us filled the living room chairs and couch and floor of Mike and Jenn's apartment with our feet up on unpacked boxes. Two of us slept while two of us watched the news for most of the night. I had become a television junky. I needed to know if I should run again. In the morning we'd be gone and we'd be safe. But for this night, I would stand guard. In only a few short hours we would head across the George Washington Bridge and be away from Manhattan.

The fear in the city continued. Late in the evening a local news station (where we got most of our very current news) reported that a truck filled with explosives had been stopped at the George Washington Bridge. Our escape route had been compromised. What would we do? We were not safe. In the morning we all got up, called friends and family, and went to buy comfortable clothes. I was still in my dress and fabulous shoes. After buying running shoes, T-shirts, and shorts we headed back to the flat to watch for an update on bridge and tunnel openings.

As I crossed the street on my way back from shopping, I saw a Baptist church on the corner and went in to pray and give thanks. It was a wonderful moment of calm. I took out the pew Bible and read Psalm 23. The words, "I will fear no evil," leapt off the page. "I will fear no evil. I will fear no evil." I went on to read Psalm 24 and read them both over and over. I gave thanks. I prayed. I cried. I left and went back to the apartment and was welcomed with good news—the bridges were open. We were free! We packed, hugged, thanked, and left. It was another beautiful day with not a cloud in the sky. As we drove over the bridge, once again we cried, this time from relief.

After crossing over the bridge, we headed down the eastern bank of New Jersey. Ashen-colored smoke billowed up into the bright blue sky. There was an eerie silence in our car until someone in the back seat said, "Look over there at the smoke. I wonder what's burning?" I glanced in my rearview mirror and saw my colleague just looking around, calmly commenting as if she had just seen a butterfly float past the window. I told her that it was the towers burning. She queried, "Still?" The towers burned until mid-January 2002.

> The enormity of the situation was too much for our cognitive brains to compute.

I tell you that story of my friend because it is important for people who weren't there to understand how little information was available to the people who were there that day. The enormity of the situation was too much for our cognitive brains to compute. That left us all asking questions such as: "I wonder what that smoke is?" Our minds had a remarkable way of protecting us during those first days.

We arrived at the hotel where we were to meet the Kellogg Canada team and were shocked to see that it was attached to Penn Station. We had heard that Grand Central station and Penn station were serious potential targets. We hesitantly parked the car, unloaded, and went in to see our Canadian rescuer and his driver. They had been on the road since 1:00 A.M. that morning. It was now approximately 1:00 P.M. They drove all the way from Canada to pick us up. Can you imagine? The rest of the group had lunch together, but I went to my room, ordered a sandwich, and called the office to see if they had heard from Ian. He was on the train headed for home. His cell phone was dead.

Fifteen minutes later, my colleagues banged on my door and said, "Quick, get your bag. There are bombs at Penn Station, we have to evacuate, the bomb squad is everywhere, and we have to get out of here. NOW!"

We ran and threw our stuff into the new car from Canada. As we slowly moved up the street in traffic, the buildings in front and behind us were being evacuated. People were running like ants out of an anthill. We held our breath.

We drove on and on until we reached Albany, New York. Kellogg had booked rooms for us there and guided us in. I came crashing down. I had my first shower since this all began and ordered a sandwich—again! It was the first food I had had in two harrowing days. The others went out for dinner and talked. And talked. And talked. And cried. I watched CNN.

Ian called at 11:30 P.M. *He was in Canada!* We talked and talked and talked. It was the first time we really had talked since the terror began. He reassured me that tomorrow we would be together. Tomorrow I would be home. The borders to Canada were open again, and I would be home. Safe.

Our team met at 6:45 A.M. in the hotel lobby and headed on our seven-hour journey north to a country that was not at war. We traveled in silence and only stopped for coffee, bathrooms, and to stretch. When I arrived home and walked through the front door, I was literally run over and knocked to the ground by Spencer as he threw his arms around me and hugged me. Although my parents had done a good job of keeping him away from the news, we did not know until many months later that he had been told of the tragedy by the neighbor's children. He knew but didn't say anything to my parents. My seven year old carried that burden alone until I walked in the door. We both cried tears of fear, tears of pain, tears of joy.

Ian was lying down trying to get some rest, as he too had not slept in days. I went into the bedroom, hugged him, and cried. When Chloe awoke, she was so excited to see me. It was just a pleasure to see her bounce, her beautiful smile, her naiveté, her spirit. We hugged, but I couldn't cry with her. I just smiled. She filled my heart with joy.

> I was home, safe and sound, but I couldn't sleep and I couldn't eat.

I was home, safe and sound, but I couldn't sleep and I couldn't eat. I became completely paranoid. I had a television installed in almost every room in our house and in my office at ONYX so that I could know what was happening in the world. I felt the need to be prepared for a great long-term tragedy. I bought $1,000 worth of emergency supplies and stored them in my parent's cellar at their cottage. I had an emergency evacuation plan with keys for each vehicle and every cottage door and a communication strategy should our family get separated. I had medication to counteract anthrax, enough for the whole family. I was a different person.

My story of 9/11 may not be anything compared to tens of thousands of others who were there that day, but 9/11 was the day that my life took a dramatic turn. It was the day that put me on a path that I could never have imagined.

9/11 changed my world forever.

Chapter Two

CHRISTMAS IN BED

It seemed like the Christmas season came only days after I returned home rather than three months later. I didn't spend any time preparing for the festive season, but rather focused on installing those TVs in every room in my house and office so that I could keep the news on all the time and know immediately when the attacks began again. I lived in total fear and paranoia.

The Christmas season was bleak. I began to slide into a deep depression. I slid down that slippery slope right into bed for two solid weeks. Our home had a seven-year-old and a five-year-old and a mommy who didn't want to get out of bed to participate in Christmas or life. I felt as if I was lying on the bottom of a swimming pool looking up at the clear, blue sky above the surface of the water.

Although I was in bed, unfortunately, I couldn't sleep all the time, so I read. The first book I picked up was Rick Warren's book, *A Purpose Driven Life*. Chapter One was painless and only a few pages long. The second chapter was titled "You Are not an Accident." Well, Mr. Warren (whoever you are), you are wrong, because I happen to know with great certainty that I *am* an accident. You see, I am adopted. *And* I have a half-sister, Marie, who recently found me while searching for her birth mother and birth father. (We share the same birth mother.) Marie had met our birth mother. She informed me that she had been only fifteen years old when she got pregnant with me. So there, Mr. Warren, I clearly was an accident. Now, don't get me wrong. I believe that God can use accidents. He can use whomever and whatever He likes whenever He likes to. But for me, I am an accident.

I wanted to be sure that Chapter Two of his book was all incorrect so that I could put the book down and move on to a Clive Cussler novel or something like that, so I read on. He went on to quote scripture that said, "You saw me before I was born and scheduled each day of my life before I began to breathe. Every day was recorded in your Book!" (Psalm 139:16). I was scheduled?

Then I read, "I am your creator. You were in my care even before you were born" (Isaiah 44:2). Really? By the end of the third page of Chapter Two, I was perplexed. I am a believer. I do believe in the Bible and that it is the inspired Word of God. So, if that is all true, then how do I reconcile the fact that I know I am an accident (based on the events at the time of my conception) and the truth that God had planned me from before the earth began (Ephesians 1:4). Hmm. I was stumped.

I began to think that *if* it is true that God had me planned, imagine what He had to do to allow the circumstances for a fifteen-year-old girl, from a small town Northern Ontario in 1963, to have sex and get pregnant. Further, I learned from Marie, that when the pregnancy was discovered, my birth mother was initially locked in her house and then banished from her family. Later she was sent 400 miles away . . . in secret . . . on a train to a house of shame—a home for unwed teenage mothers. She had humiliated her father. In fact, he told her that she had "ruined his life." My birth mother was an only child, and my birth grandparents had great expectations of her going to a teacher's college, marrying, and having 3.5 children (the average back in that day). All of this was lost because of me. Their dreams were shattered. Their hope was gone. And so was their only child.

I was overcome with the hurt, the shame, the guilt, and the pain that must have been felt by everyone involved. Could God really have planned this? Is it possible that I was not an accident? I hadn't realized until that moment that I had felt like a mistake my whole life. I was raised by a loving, Christian adopted family as an only child. They loved me and cared for me and always made me feel special, wanted, and *chosen!* I wasn't just one of those babies (like you, maybe) who was *just* born into the family. You know, you get whatever pops out. Oh no, Mom and Dad went to the baby store and "chose me" out of all the babies that were for sale that day. I was special and they made sure that I knew it. Despite their sales pitch and their attempt to make me feel like a member of the family, I was still a mistake, an accident. Or so I thought until the age of thirty-eight when it all started to crumble because of this guy, this author, who said I wasn't . . . a mistake.

The logical part of my brain told me as I lay in bed that day that *if* I believe the Bible to be true (and I do), and *if* it tells me in all those scriptures that I am not an accident (and it does), and *if* I am not an accident (I'm repeating myself here for my own benefit), and *if* God allowed all the pain and suffering and shame and guilt to happen so that I am here (and He did) . . . Wow! A moment of pause. If He allowed these things to happen so that I am here, I had better giddee up and find out what on earth He brought me here for. The Bible says, "The Lord will fill me with His purpose" (Psalm 138:8). That's what I needed! His purpose. I realized that lying in bed in a depressed state wasn't likely my purpose in

---

Please note my childish thought process. We really don't do that in Canada.

> I realized that lying in bed in a depressed state wasn't likely my purpose in life so I leapt out of bed, full of the vim and vigor.

life so I leapt out of bed, full of the vim and vigor. I knew that I had a purpose and couldn't wait to have it revealed!

Well, my vim and vigor lasted less than a day. It seemed that my new-found purpose of finding my purpose wasn't enough to keep me afloat. I went to my doctor who put me on anti-depression medication that allowed me to float to the surface of the pool from time to time. I had a few good days, and then my head seemed to sink back below the surface where I again looked up at the blue sky from below. I went back to my doctor several months later. He doubled my medication, and voila! My head was above the surface, I could see the sky, and I could breathe the clean air.

I don't remember much of 2002. It was not really a blur, I just don't remember it. I know from my accounting records at work that we had a good year. Business was good, but I was numb and detached. I do remember having a conversation with God about Him sending me to Africa to be a missionary. I thought that sounded like a worthy purpose. It was something I had always thought would be cool. I asked and asked Him to send me, then one day He answered. It was the strangest thing.

Now I had sort of heard God before. There were things I just seemed to know that He wanted me to do after praying, but this time I *heard* Him. It wasn't an audible answer, but it was definitely Him. So my question was, "God, why don't you send me to Africa to talk to the people?" His answer was short and clear. He said, "What would you say to them?" I was stunned. What a good question. What would I say? It's not like I had ever really read my Bible so I couldn't really encourage them with scripture or give them the Word of God to tell them what to do. I didn't know a thing about poverty or injustice. I couldn't preach if my life depended on it. Well, I could lecture, but those lectures wouldn't necessarily be very encouraging in tone or content. And so I asked myself what I would say. I have nothing to say to a continent of people dying from hunger, AIDS, and injustice. How sad was that? I was as prepared to give a word of encouragement or advice to the president of a multi-national company as to a cab driver in New York City. But what would I say in Africa? I had nothing. I immediately decided that I had better start reading my Bible. At least then I would have a clue. And so I began.

My "Bible reading goal," because that's just the way I am, was to read the whole thing in a year. And I did it. It was amazing. I had heard just about every story in the Bible in Sunday school or church, but I hadn't heard them in order. I knew that Jesus had fed a crowd a few loaves and fishes, but I had no idea that he did it twice. That was a big deal to me. I don't know why, but it was. I will admit that it was discipline that got me through reading the whole Bible and not a love for scripture. Don't get me wrong. There were a few stories, scriptures, verses, and proverbs that made me say "Ah-ha!" But the general reading was just plain discipline. And I did it! Whoo hoo! Now I could say "hallelujah" with a reason (not that I had ever used that word before). Now I was ready for Africa. "Put me in coach, I'm ready!" Oh, how naïve I was. I hope God smiled and didn't just shake His head.

Chapter Three

A BOY NAMED KANTWA

One Monday morning in the middle of March, 2003, I was invited to be a guest on a Canadian Christian television program called 100 Huntley Street. Apparently their Wednesday guest had cancelled unexpectedly, and they needed someone to enter a discussion on "tithing." It was odd because I had only been on the program once before, but I was on the phone with the right person at the right time and the invitation was given. Tithing happened to be a favorite topic of mine, so I agreed. But a discussion on tithing was not to be the important part of that day, at least not to me.

During the program, I sat beside Reynold Mainse, the VP of Missions for Crossroads (the parent company of 100 Huntley Street). Reynold and I had gone to Evangel University in Springfield, Missouri, together in the early 80s, but had not kept in contact over the years, so I was so excited to hear about his adventures in missions around the world. I asked why he had never invited me to join him and his wife, Kathy, on a missions trip.

It was a ridiculous question coming from what I affectionately called myself ("the capitalist-pig") to the missionary whom I hadn't seen in eighteen years. He politely responded that he would never have guessed I would be interested in doing missions work. How wrong he was! I was looking for my purpose and surely God could use me in the mission field. After all, Matthew 28, "The Great Commission" tells us to *go.* And so I wanted to go, and told him so. Reynold said okay. Four weeks later I flew with his wife Kathy to Zambia, to meet Reynold who was just coming out of Southern Sudan. My journey had begun.

I knew that Africa was not a part of my purpose, but I was hoping I could clear my head there, gain perspective, and come back refreshed and ready to take on the challenges of the day. What was our mission? Reynold and Kathy were there to film the "street kids." I had never heard of them. Apparently there are children, thousands of them, living on the streets in many African countries because their parents have died.

For the first time since I could remember, I had no official role. I wasn't leading the trip, so I wasn't responsible for anything (other than my malaria pills, tucking in my mosquito netting, and not drinking the water or eating anything that had touched the water). I wasn't very well qualified to do "nothing." I hadn't done "nothing" since I was a very small child. However, as I sat quietly and observed all that was going on around me my life began to change forever.

> I wasn't very well qualified to do "nothing." I hadn't done "nothing" since I was a very small child.

When we arrived in Lusaka, Zambia, we were transported to our hotel—an HIV/AIDS Testing Center. You must understand that I was used to staying at the Four Seasons Hotels. And to my knowledge there is no AIDS testing done at any of their fifty-five exclusive properties worldwide. We took our bags to our rooms and surveyed the premises. I stepped aside when the hotel officials came in, closed the window, wrapped my bed in mosquito netting (including tucking the netting under the mattress so that "things" did not crawl up and in), and then sprayed my room with tons of bug spray. They asked me to leave the room with them so they could close the door and let things die. Hmmm.

After a delicious meal and a meeting with our host, Bishop Joshua Banda, we sat waiting for our driver. Chite was the young man who would safely take us out on the streets of Lusaka to meet the street kids. It was safe with him because the children knew his face and his heart (and his van that was clearly marked "Lazarus Project" on the side).

Lusaka is a city of two million people in a country of ten million. The streets of Lusaka are home to street kids—orphans and vulnerable children who roam the streets picking through garbage bins for the rotten leftovers from the poor in town. They have no access to a bathroom, a shower, fresh food, education, or parents. Many of them have been orphaned by the AIDS pandemic. Just as many have run away from home as young as six years old to avoid the daily beatings by their mother or one of her men callers.

That night was the first night of my life. I knew nothing before that night. I didn't exist. We left late in the evening as the children do not "bunk down" until after 10:00 P.M. At every corner we saw large piles of garbage lying along the sidewalk in a strange yet orderly fashion. Chite pulled over and stopped beside one of the piles.

The night was very dark and I squinted to see what I was looking at. As we stepped out, my eyes focused and I saw the garbage move. It was just a rustle—a flash of motion and then it was gone. Were they rats? Was it a snake? And then at the other end of the pile, another movement. And then I saw it. A head. A tiny little jet black head poked

> This was not a pile of garbage. These were children, carefully wrapped in garbage to keep the cold away.

up from under the pile. This was not a pile of garbage. These were children, carefully wrapped in garbage to keep the cold away. They were lying closely together in a tight "spoon in the drawer" type formation to keep warm. The temperature was close to 50 degrees Fahrenheit that night and I was thankful for my jacket. I stared. I could not move. It must be a dream. This is not possible.

Immediately I thought, "Well, we will just have to get them to a home. This can't go on like this. Surely I can raise the funds to take them in. Obviously, people do not know that these poor children are here. *That* must be why I am here. To arrange to have these children brought in off the street." I did not know until later that night that it was estimated that there were 75,000 street children in Zambia alone.

At this site, there were in total, a dozen boys lying together. They were so drowsy they could hardly wake up to speak to us. This journey has one of those "don't try this at home, folks" warnings attached to it. These boys are very dangerous. They steal, they stab, they kill, they rape, they destroy. But they are boys. They are children, few of them above the age of fifteen, some as young as seven.

As it turns out these boys could not wake up because they were in a drug-induced sleep. You see, the kids will eat from garbage bins and steal food to survive, but the money that they can beg from strangers is held exclusively for *bostik*, their warm blanket on a cold night. We were able to rouse a couple of them long enough for them to tell us who they were, how they came to the street, and what bostik was.

Bostik is a "wonderful" combination of gasoline (petrol) and glue. It is not as good with one ingredient and not the other, but one will suffice better than none at all. For a few Kwatcha (just pennies) children can buy these ingredients and put them in a plastic PVC bottle (like our small water bottles) and this becomes their comfort for the night. In fact, they carry these bottles with them day and night, stuck in the cuff of their shirt sleeve or in a front pocket. Once they have mixed the magic together they will put their mouths over the mouth of the bottle and take a big deep breath. The fumes go straight to their lungs and then to their heads.

This magic potion is critical to their survival. (Sounds crazy doesn't it? But it is.) Bostik helps the children forget. They forget that they have not eaten in two days. They forget that they were raped twice yesterday and three times the day before. They forget that their skin is crawling with lice and fleas. They forget that the police caught them and beat them with sticks last time they got caught stealing an orange. They forget that their father died in front of them after their mother had sat and nursed him day and night. They forget when their mother was too weak to get up and go to the bathroom and when they had to fetch water and clean her private areas for months until she finally died. But that is not all. Bostik helps them forget the day their mom couldn't drink water anymore because the sores in her mouth (thrush) were bleeding and oozing out on to her face and she could not speak—not even to cry.

But bostik will never let them forget the day their mother finally died. She had been sick for many months and hadn't been up at all. She hadn't eaten real food in weeks and was in too much pain to drink. She was so thin and dehydrated that she had no tears to cry as they sat around and watched for every breath she took. No drug would ever let them for-get the women who came howling and crying when they were called in with the news of her death. Nor could they forget being told that they had to go to a coffin maker and buy a coffin. With what money? Who knew? They placed her in the box and sat through the day-long funeral, but not even sleep could take away the memories of seven brothers and sisters huddling together on a mud floor, hungry that first night in the dark, wondering what tomorrow held. It wasn't as if they had a full refrigerator and after that when the food was gone they would have to find work. There were two or three cups of Nshima (mealie meal, a cornmeal porridge), enough for a few days if they didn't eat much. And then what would they do. Seven children under the age of ten. Alone. And two of the little ones had bad coughs and couldn't eat much.

Bostik was "good." It was a magic drug for these children. Even after we learned what it was, we wouldn't dare tell them to stop taking it, though we knew that it was frying their brains and killing their bodies. Who would be so cruel as to leave them alone on the street with their reality and their memories without a crutch? Not me.

We thanked the boys for sharing their lives with us and we shared bread and juice with them. They sat up and watched us drive away as if they had just had a really weird dream. We moved on and visited many "piles" of children that night, young and old (up to age eighteen), dirty and sick, wounded and bleeding. And then we turned the corner and saw him.

It was the last stop of the night for us. These boys had found a sheltered space with light to keep them safe (or safer). The wall was painted bright yellow and someone had painted all the grouting red. An exposed light bulb hanging above their heads illuminated the yellow and red brick and made it look like an animated cartoon drawing. The same pile of boys wrapped in garbage was lined up along the wall, but one boy sat up looking around. We got out of the van and locked it up tightly. Then we approached this young boy. His name was Kantwa.

Kantwa was the saddest person I have ever seen in my life. He was a tiny boy for his age of nine years. He was quiet and timid, but seemingly unafraid of the strangers approaching him in the dead of night. His hands were tucked between his bare knees to keep them warm but his

> Kantwa was the saddest person I have ever seen in my life.

bare feet were exposed to the night air. Chite asked the boy to tell us his story. Over a period of an hour, this is what he told us about his life:

> When I was only six years old both my parents died within months of each other. My older brother (aged eight) and I lived alone for a short while in our home until some relatives came along and told us we had to leave. They said they needed the home for their large family and that we must go to the city and find a relative or someone to care for us. They kicked us out right then and there with nothing but a few Kwatcha to pay for the bus ride. My brother and I were afraid, but we got on the bus (for the first time ever) and got off when we arrived in the city (Lusaka). It was a cold, dark night as I held onto my brother's hand getting out of the bus. My eyes could not believe what they were seeing. I had never been in a town before. I had never seen so many people. I had never seen buildings like that. There were many people pushing and shoving us and my brother's hand slipped out of mine. That was the last time I saw him.

Kantwa spoke in such soft tones that it was amazing Chite could even hear him to translate this story to us. I felt as if

I was in a dream. This was Hollywood. No truth could be stranger than this fiction I was hearing. The boy continued:

> I found a bench near a wall and sat on it. I waited there for my brother to come back. I waited all night and then all day and then the second night. My brother never came back. But some other boys did. They invited me to come with them, to join them on the street in their family. I said "No, I must wait for my brother," and they told me he would not be coming for me. That was the night I became a street boy.

We later found out that this was also the night that Kantwa was raped repeatedly by the older boys as he became their sex slave. He would be the one stuffed through small broken windows to let the older boys in the front doors to rob the houses. He would be the one forced to pick through the worst of the garbage bins when there was no food for the family. By the time we met Kantwa he had been living this life for three years.

I wanted to throw up. What could we do? I touched his legs and they were freezing cold. His knees were calloused and thick like an elephant's skin. I did not know what to do. I couldn't think or process what I was seeing and hearing. I could only be there in the present with him. I held his hand so he could feel the touch of a mother's hand on his if only for a moment. I wanted to look into his eyes and tell him that everything would be okay, but I knew my eyes would deceive me, so I just looked at him with love. I tried to give a sense of hopefulness, even when there was none evident to any of us. He smiled. I couldn't believe it. His little eyes brightened for a moment, and he smiled. It was time to leave and I didn't know what to do. I went to the van and quickly took off my shoes and socks and went back to him, putting the socks on his frigid feet. He smiled and then looked down the pile with concern to where the older boys were sleeping. I knew instinctively what the problem was. The boys would beat him for those socks. Was it worth putting him in more risk for this small gift? We spoke to Chite and he went down to the end and spoke to two of the older boys who had awakened while we were there. He asked them to protect Kantwa and the socks and not to let anyone else steal them or hurt him for them. They assured Chite that they would fulfill his wishes. I do not know if they did, but my heart tells me he was in jeopardy for my actions. Then we left.

We just left. We left all those boys lying on the concrete, wrapped in shreds of garbage and went back to our palace to sleep. But sleep never came.

What kind of God allows this to happen? What kind of God sits back and lets his kids be treated worse than animals? I couldn't sleep. I couldn't think. I couldn't breath. I couldn't listen to music. The next morning I told my hosts that we must go and get Kantwa and bring him in off the street. I could not leave Zambia without at least one child saved. The answer, sadly, was no. There

> What kind of God sits back and lets his kids be treated worse than animals?

was no room in the home. The Lazarus Project was home to fifty-five boys with space for only thirty-five. They simply could not take another one. There was no space.

I went crazy. How can there not be space for just one more. But I knew they spoke the truth. Some of the boys slept two to a bed, some on the floor, and it was true, there was no space to move about. But Kantwa was little, he wouldn't take much room. Reynold and Kathy had been equally struck by Kantwa and wanted to do something, but what? I don't know what we did that day or the next. I have no recollection of doing anything but think about Kantwa. I tried to write in my journal, but there were no words to express my anguish, my shock, my horror at what I was seeing. I was so used to being in control of things. I was so used to making things happen at work and in life. If I can have four million packs of Trident gum hand-packed into little plastic sleeves in a week to hang on two-litre bottles of 7UP, *surely* I could figure out a way to get this child off the street.

It was hopeless. I was hopeless. And yet Kantwa didn't appear hopeless. Was I feeling sorrier for me than for him? Was my rage and anger targeted at my inability to "fix it" rather than at the fact that he was left as garbage on the street? I sat down and tried to write again and a poem came out. (I have only written one poem in my life before this time and that was in the second grade. It was called "Maurice the Brontosaurus" because I was mad at my friend named Maurice. I got in so much trouble for writing it that I gave up poetry for good. This one just seemed to slip out onto the page.)

Hope for the Hopeless

What happens to the human soul
when there is no hope?
Does it fight to find light?
Does it settle for a life of darkness and fear?

In Zambia, the street boys find hope
even when there is no hope.

The yellow streetlight provides
a wonderfully illuminated safe haven.
The smell of urine and filth is as
comforting and familiar as the smell of freshly-baked bread.
The daily beatings and sexual abuse
ensure that there is regular human touch.
The garbage cans guarantee that
no one will go to sleep hungry.

You see?
There is hope for the hopeless.

Two days later (it seemed like two years) we were told that the Lazarus Project was going to make space for Kantwa. I don't know how they did it, but they did, and our next challenge would begin that night. Now we had to go back to the street and try to find this one boy.

The day passed and evening came. Filled with great anticipation, we piled into the car. We were warned that it was highly unlikely we would find Kantwa again in a city with so many kids just like him, but we would try. I was so hopeful. He was ours! We went to the city center and turned onto the street where Kantwa had last been seen. As we approached the yellow and red wall, my breathing stopped again. As we pulled up and stopped the van, we knew we needed to pray. When we finished our prayer, we left the van to find Kantwa. I hopefully scanned the familiar place where I had last seen him.

There he was! He was sitting just where we left him, leaning against the wall while all the others slept. He seemed to recognize us, but was not surprised, alarmed, or happy that we had come back. Chite bent down and asked him if he knew about the Lazarus Project Home for Boys. He said he did. Chite asked if he wanted to come and live at that home where he would be safe, get clean food, clean clothes, sleep in a bed, and get an education. Somewhat hesitantly he said he did. Chite then told him that he could choose two friends to come with him.

We couldn't believe our ears! We were bringing in three little boys from the street. They would be safe and saved! He smiled and went to make his choice from his sleeping friends. He carefully chose two and tried to shake them awake. They would not stir. They were so drugged with the bostik they had inhaled that he was unable to wake them. Chite reached into the pile and pulled them out by their jackets.

> We were bringing in three little boys from the street. They would be safe and saved!

Finally, the boys roused to hear the news. It was unbelievable. A miracle had happened. Although it was irrelevant to what was happening, I couldn't help but notice that Kantwa's new socks were gone. I asked Chite to ask him where they had gone. Had they been stolen? Had he been hurt? Had the boys raped him as punishment for his treasure? It was then I saw into Kantwa's heart. He looked at me and grinned from ear to ear and said, "Oh, don't worry. They didn't get the socks. I hid them far from here in a safe place where no one will ever find them." He was proud. He was smart. I went blank.

The socks that I gave him to keep him warm from the cold night air were tucked safely away in a special place where only he could go and look at them. They were his hidden treasure. Never to be worn, except in secret. Never to be seen by anyone but him. Never to be stolen by anyone . . . ever. It just didn't make sense that he would do this, but then a still, small voice asked me how many treasures I had been given that I had hidden away. Not only the "good china" that sat unused for fear of being broken, the good wine that was kept for a "special occasion," or the good gifts that I had been given from above that I was not using for their correct purpose. Kantwa was, in fact, using the socks for encouragement. He had a secret that could spur him on when times were really tough. He could sneak off to find the socks, and he could hold them and admire them and smell them (they were reasonably clean when they were given to him), and he could even try them on from time to time if he dared. But he would never use them for the purpose for which they were intended.

I sat and wondered. How many gifts does God give us that we keep tucked away as our little secret? Do you have the gift of singing, but only do it in the shower? Do you have the gift of wisdom, but assuredly keep that wisdom to yourself? Do you have the gift of discernment, but save it for you and your business? Are you like Kantwa and his socks?

We loaded the three boys into the van and wrapped them in brand new wool blankets that had been purchased just for that special night. I crawled into the back seat and reached out to receive each little boy onto the seat beside me. Reynold was capturing the whole story on video camera. Kathy was trying to maintain control as she told the story on film. I was in my glory with Kantwa on my lap and the other two bundled on either side of me.

The night was very dark as it always is in Africa. We drove through the streets and out into the country for our journey to safety. An occasional street light illuminated the inside of the van as we drove, and I did not miss the silhouette of many "creatures" jumping for joy and jumping off the boys heads onto the nice clean blanket. I held my breath, held them tighter, and held back the tears. We drove in silence and disbelief at what we were witnessing.

> It was resurrection morning and these boys had just been raised from the dead.

After many minutes the silence was broken with a simple question asked by Kathy.

"What day is it?" she asked. The answer was Sunday morning at 12:20 A.M.

She said, "It's Easter morning." The dam broke and the tears poured. It was resurrection morning and these boys had just been raised from the dead. I had been there. I had been a witness to the greatness of God and His mercy. But we only had three. What about the rest? I settled into the darkness with my boys. The rest would have to wait, for now was the time for rejoicing.

We later learned that children are often plucked off the street and sold or given to brothels (or simply to bad people) to use, abuse, and discard. Kantwa's initial hesitancy was that he really did not know where we were taking him. When he saw that we had told the truth, he was not only relieved, but he was speechless.

Chapter Four

A PLACE CALLED KIPSONGO

We left Zambia a day later and flew to Nairobi, Kenya where we were met by a Kenyan family named Mully. Charles Mully, known as Mully, and Esther Mully are the founders of the Mully Children's Family Home (MCF) which is home to hundreds of Kenyan street children just like Kantwa. Mully himself was abandoned by his parents when he was only six years old and lived on the street for many years. Through a local missionary who cared for street boys, Mully learned about the love of God and made a life-long commitment to follow Jesus while still a teenager. That decision changed his life, and the Lord blessed him.

Mully had lived from day to day, eating from the garbage cans outside the wealthy homes in Nairobi. He would steal or beg to survive. One day when he was a teenager and had hit rock bottom, he knocked on the gate of a big house and begged the woman to let him in and to give him food. The woman allowed him through the gate and into her home. She fed him and gave him water, and then asked him if he wanted to work. Mully was so excited. He worked in her garden, did jobs around the house, did her dishes and laundry, and proved himself to be a great worker.

After many months the woman asked her husband if he could get Mully a job at the coffee bean farm where he worked. The husband agreed, and Mully began to work in the field. Eventually, he became the overseer and ended up in the office learning how to do the books. This uneducated street child was working hard, learning fast, loving God, and being trained for future work. Mully was able to save some money and bought himself a *matatu* (taxi). He worked all day at the farm and then drove his taxi at night and on weekends to make more money.

During the next several years Mully met and married Esther, and they began a family, ending with eight children. Mully left the farm and now was the proud owner of a taxi company, a luxury bus company called Mullyways, a tire and car parts distribution company, a petrol company, and a car insurance company. Mully had become a very important and wealthy man in the town of Eldoret. His children were in private school, they dressed in the best clothes, and he was a deacon at his church. He even helped fund and build the large sanctuary that is there today. There was no doubt that Mully had made it. God had blessed him beyond his wildest imagination—rags to riches—that was the real life story of Charles Mully.

One day Mully had driven to Nairobi in his brand new Mercedes Benz to do some business. As he parked on the road and stepped out of his car, he was greeted by a group of street boys who offered to watch over his car while he went into his meeting. Mully knew that street boys did this to make money so that they could buy more glue to sniff or cigarettes to smoke, so he refused their offer. Thirty minutes later Mully came back to his car only to find it missing. The new Mercedes Benz was nowhere to be seen, but one boy sat where the car once rested. Mully was shocked and asked the boy where his car had gone. The boy responded with a shrug and the reminder that he had not been paid to care for the car. Mully's new car was never found.

Mully got in a taxi packed with people, animals, and vegetables and traveled the five-hour journey back to his home in Eldoret. On his trip the Lord tapped him on the shoulder and reminded him that he was once one of those street boys. Mully had been the one there begging for money. Mully had been the one without parental love, food, or education. Mully would still be there if God had not shone down His mercy and grace and changed Mully's life. The Lord said to him, "I have given you all that you have. Now it is time to give it back."

The details of Mully's story I will leave for you to read in his own biography titled *Father to the Fatherless*. However, I will say that Mully was obedient. Over the next three years he sold his business, changed the lifestyle of his family, and started to bring street kids to live in their home.

By the time Reynold, Kathy, and I got to meet Mully and Esther, they had been running the home for thirteen years and had more than 500 children living there. Their home for small children (approximately seventy) was still in their original home in Eldoret. The older children (approximately 400) were living on beautiful farm property in Ndalani plus a home for teenage street girls was being built in a region called Yatta. It would house 200 very troubled teenage prostitutes within a year.

As Reynold was there to film the street children's situation and show where there was hope, Mully felt it best that we start at the beginning— a very good place to start. We got in a van and drove to the slums in Kitale—to a place called Kipsongo. This is where many of the street children have run to, and from where many of Mully's children have been rescued.

As we drove into the town, the stench that came through our closed windows made my stomach lurch.

Kitale is a town that is fifty kilometers from the Ugandan border. It has a population of 25,000 people and 18,000 of those live in Kipsongo—the slum. As we drove into the town, the stench that came through our closed windows made my stomach lurch. I asked if we were in the slum and was told that it was still several kilometers away. I didn't know if I could make it any closer. I reached into my fanny pack and removed a Listerine pocket pack, tore off a small corner, licked it, and stuck it up my nostril (not recommended usage). It did help. We drove through the town and stopped on the side of the road, and we were there. It was the rainy season, so everything was very wet and slippery and smelly. We stepped out into the red African mud and left holes in a path behind us, as two inches of mud stuck to all sides of our running shoes.

There was a group of teenagers from MCF who had gone ahead of us to Kipsongo in order to get permission from the village chief for us to enter the area. It is a very dangerous place, and we were told that we would be killed quickly if we ventured in alone. We had many things going against us: we were strangers, we were white, and we had cameras. At that time the government of Kenya denied that there were slums in Kenya, so photography was not allowed. The chief gave his permission and we entered a land I could never have prepared for. We slipped through a tiny alleyway that appeared to be the entrance to a group of homes. Each home was carefully constructed and yet appeared fragile and ready to blow away. The people used long sticks and twigs to create the frame of each house, much like the Native American Indians would have built a tepee. The difference was that once the frame was built here in Kipsongo; there were no skins to wrap around the home. Here the women would use plastic garbage bags or old torn clothes or whatever they could find and tie it to the wood in order to keep out the rain and sun. Each hut was a mosaic of very dirty, once-colored garbage.

Each layer told a different tale of history, like the layers of wallpaper in an old kitchen.

My homemade nasal insert was starting to wear off. The smell of urine and feces mixed with wet ground and garbage-covered homes made my stomach flip again. Beside me a small boy squatted down next to a small flow of water in the middle of our path and began to defecate. He had no underpants so the movement was quick and decisive. As a mother, I immediately asked where the toilet was so that I could take this child there. I was quickly informed that there was no toilet. I informed them that there were 18,000 people living in Kipsongo (as if they were completely unaware of how many people lived in their hometown) and there *had* to be a toilet somewhere. The woman with me shook her head no.

I wasn't satisfied; they clearly did not understand what I was saying. However, they had understood all too well and were correct in their information. The 18,000 inhabitants of Kipsongo did not have a single toilet, outhouse, or pit latrine. They were squatters on land they did not own, so no one had ever invested the time to dig a deep hole. I asked the woman where she "did her business." She explained that she went in the corn field, and her husband usually went over "there" and pointed. The kids go wherever they are when they need to go, like the little boy who had just finished his business and stood back up beside me and took my hand. I looked around behind me and found a woman with a small can, collecting water from this same little trickle of water I was standing in—right where the boy had defecated. Where was I? What was I doing here? This was crazy! My head

> The 18,000 inhabitants of Kipsongo did not have a single toilet, outhouse, or pit latrine.

was spinning. There was no way to turn, nowhere to go, no way to hide. At the end of the day I would end up back at MCF in a clean bed, with hot food, and my own toilet, but these people would never see any of these things. Where was God in the slums of Kipsongo?

We heard stories that day of young girls who were prostitutes at the age of nine, offering sex for food. We heard stories of young teenagers giving birth on the mud streets and then taking the babies and throwing them in the "forest" (which was really a place of reeds and tall grass) because they had nothing to feed them and didn't want "it" anyway. We met children who were as young as three years old, living alone, going from house to house looking for their daily bread. We learned that there were thirteen types of skin diseases that if left untreated, can be fatal. We saw the face of tuberculosis and cholera and AIDS. But in those same faces we saw joy. I didn't know where it came from or why it was there, but they had joy.

That day as we left the slums, Mully rescued several people: a four-day-old baby that was about to be thrown away, her mother, and a handful of other children who were in desperate conditions. This "father to the fatherless" became a new dad, nine times over again. When I got back to MCF that night, I disinfected my shoes and clothes as instructed, and then showered and came down for dinner. How could I eat after seeing what I had seen? How could I sleep again without seeing the faces of the children, the empty eyes of the old women, and the black eyes of the male predators who just stood back and watched? When I crawled into bed that night and tried to write about what I had seen, once again, my thoughts came out as a poem, only my third one ever.

Death Trap

The eyes of the old have seen it all.
They look right through us as if we weren't there.
They are dead to the pain and dead to the world.
And yet they're alive.

The eyes of the young are sickly and wide,
filled with hope, and tears and crust and infection.
They are dead to their mothers.
And yet they're alive.

The eyes of the big boys are glazed and harsh.
They glare at the girls, the big and the small.
They are predators whose victims wish they were dead.
And yet they're alive.

The eyes of the girls are filled with fear.
They know abandonment and sickness and rape and pain.
They plead to be taken so that they won't die,
so that they will live.

The eyes of the forest have witnessed much death,
from the dead to the dying, from the young to the unborn.
These are dead, they have been forgotten
As if they had never lived.

The eyes of Jesus don't miss a thing.
They are sad and tear-filled for each little child.
But the eyes of the Father are loving and kind.
He sent His child, so that all these may live.

Several days later I met a boy named Paul who had been brought from Kipsongo to the home when he was a small boy. When I met Paul, he was playing soccer with the other boys in Ndalani. He ran and kicked and played very well, considering he had only one foot. Paul used a crutch to support his weight and ran around the soccer field as any active ten-year-old would.

When Paul was a baby, he had lived in a garbage hut with his parents who were "drunkards" as they are called in that part of the world. As happens to so many children in Africa, one night there was an accident. Paul's parents were drinking *brewe*.* After an altercation between the parents, the oil lamp lighting the hut tipped over and poured out on Paul's foot and leg, burning him very badly

Paul was only one month old at the time. His parents tried to soothe their injured child, but had no access to money or transportation to a hospital, so Paul's injury went unchecked. After five days of excruciating pain, his burns took a turn for the worse, becoming infected and beginning to turn green and to stink. His mother finally took him to the local hospital in Kitale, where he was immediately admitted. Paul's foot and leg had become gangrenous and had to be amputated.

While Paul was recovering in the hospital, two life-changing events happened. The first was that Paul contracted polio. At that time Kenya was one of the only countries in the world where polio had not been eradicated. The onset of polio greatly slowed Paul's recovery, and he stayed in the

---

*Brewe is illegal drink made by women to earn an income. It is cooked in a pot over a fire and consists of whatever the woman has access to that day including beer, petrol or paint thinner. It costs pennies to buy a cup and is highly lethal.

hospital for many months. He suffered with polio for two years.

When he was ready to be released, the second life-changing event happened. The hospital workers went to find his parents to collect him and found that his mother had died of AIDS. They took Paul back to Kipsongo and left him on the ground outside the entrance to the homes and left. Paul had many things going against him at this point: his mother was dead, he had no foot, and he was crippled due to polio. No one would want him. He would be left there to die. His father did not want to care for him and really had no means to do so. Paul's foot and polio caused him to be in and out of the hospital for the next five years.

One day Mully was in Kipsongo ministering to the people when the chief told him about Paul and his younger brother. Mully became a father again to the two boys that day. When I met Paul, he was a quiet, shy boy with a big beautiful smile. He was smart and doing well in school, loved to draw, loved to play his drum, and wanted to be a surgeon when he grew up. He could have given our son, Spencer, a run for his money in a game of soccer, even with only one foot.

Chapter Five

TRANSFORMATIONAL POWER

We had seen the slum from which many of the children had come. We had seen what we did not believe could exist. We had seen what should not exist. Now it was time to meet the children who had been rescued by Mully and were being cared for and loved in his children's home. We traveled south, past the equator, and down along the Rift Valley to Ndalani and the new location in Yatta. Our next few days were filled with meeting the children and interviewing them. We sat under giant trees, on rocks, or by the sleepy river (with one hippo and a couple of crocodiles) and heard story after story of children who had come from the streets. I sat and listened, hour after hour, to each child quietly and gently tell his or her personal story of tragedy that ended in complete and miraculous transformation and joy there at the Mully Children's Family Home. I sat and wept with each new child who sat telling a story. None of them shed a tear.

In those two days, I heard children speak of living on the street and having bigger children play a game with them while they slept. They would pick one child each night and pour gasoline on them and then light them on fire. The small child would awaken, on fire, with other menacing children pointing and laughing at them. I saw their gruesome scars. I heard many stories of children having to sit outside their hut at night in the darkness while listening to their mother prostituting herself inside so that she had money. Each morning brought hope that the monies earned would bring food, but that didn't happen very often. Cigarettes and brewe were her purchases of choice, so that she could forget the life she was living. Then there were the babies who came along year after year. Another brother, another sister, less food, less love, more beatings. It would only stop when they ran to the street.

I heard stories of small children being hog-tied upside down from a tree and beaten by their mother's boyfriend with a big stick while she threw buckets of cold water on the child for being bad. I heard horrific stories of torture and human sacrifice. I heard story after story. And they were true. Each and every one was backed with fact and files in the office in Nairobi.

One boy told me that his mother dedicated him to Satan when he was only six years old. He calmly told me how he had killed his first person, a child, later that year. His story was like a horror film. I just couldn't believe my ears. I couldn't believe that I was looking into the eyes of a seventeen-year-old boy who had killed people, worshipped Satan, and lived a life of pure evil until Mully found him.

After I finished hearing this boy's story, I was furious—Not at him or his mother or the cult that he had been pulled into. I was mad at God. How could this God whom I believed in, allow this to happen to a child? How? I had learned in church and Sunday school that my God was a loving God. He was a loving Father who cared for His children. Now, I didn't believe that. Not this God. He didn't care or He would never have allowed *any* of this to happen. These are *children*! It was *wrong*! Where was God when all of this was happening? I went back to my room because I wanted to scream. I went in and locked the door behind me. I stomped around the room, grabbed a pillow, and screamed into it (so no one could hear me and think I was nuts.) And then

I began to write. If you saw the scrawl in my journal you would see just how angry I was. And again, my writing came out as a poem. Here is what my rage said:

Where Were You GOD?

Oh God, how could You let this happen?
How could You allow such evil forces
to steal a six-year-old child?
How could You allow all of these children
to be abandoned?

Where was Your love?
Where were Your loving arms?
Where were the angels?
What were they doing?

Were they busy protecting my safe drive to the office?
Were they there helping me in that big business presentation?
Were they there when I prayed for healing of my daughter's
foot?

Let me have the car accident!
Let me fail in business!
Let Chloe's foot heal naturally!

I give You my guardian angels, Lord.
Use them to protect the children.
I beg You.
Protect the children.
They have done nothing wrong.
I have done so much.

Protect Godfrey, Lord.
Cover him with Your angels.
Please surround him with the angels
who have the biggest wing span
and the softest touch.
Pour Your love on him, Lord.
Give him my share.
I beg You.

Where was I?

I was living in a big, beautiful home, safely.
I ate in the best restaurants in the world.
I drove a Porsche, was pregnant two times with children.
I traveled the world.
I belonged to a wonderful church
that fueled me whenever I "needed" fueling.

Forgive me, Lord. Where was I?

Where was I when they were on the street?
Where was I when they had no food?
Where was I when they were being raped and beaten?

Forgive me, Lord, for I have sinned.

What do You want me to do, Lord?

Show me, I beg You. What do You want me to do?

Later that day I listened to a good-looking young man named David, aged twenty, tell me of his father's death from tuberculosis when he was only eight. His mother would beat her eight children each night and then send them away crying in the dark while she focused on her primary profession—prostitution. During the day she would make and sell illegal brewe to supplement her income. This resulted in many arrests by police and weeks in prison while her children then remained alone. When David turned nine, he decided to leave home and run to the street. I asked him what he was looking for there. He told me, "Love." I wept.

He continued his story saying that life on the street is survival of the fittest. "You must do whatever you must to survive on the street," said David. He immediately began stealing, smoking marijuana, sniffing glue, and fighting. David continued, "I was a bad boy on the street," giving me a playful smile. He told me that the police called the children "street urchins" and would chase the boys and beat them with clubs until they were unconscious, leaving them in a pool of their own blood to hopefully die. An even worse fate was when the police would arrest the boys. They would put them in jail for a few nights to abuse them and then take them to juvenile prison.* David was in and out of juvenile prison four times as a young boy. He was "very bad."

> David could not believe that this man would "lower" himself to the level of the "leftovers of creation" as he and his friends were called.

The little boys didn't only have the police to worry about. The big

---

* Juvenile prison is a state-run detention home for children who have committed a crime and must be punished. This place is home to children from toddler to age sixteen (adult). Minimum stay is three months to ensure that they are rehabilitated. Crimes can include stealing food, sleeping on porches or roaming the streets while important government officials are in town (police clean-up is known as "street-sweeping").

boys would often chase them, and once they were caught, they would gang rape them for fun. When Mully went out into the street to talk to the boys, he would play soccer with them and listen to their problems. David could not believe that this man would "lower" himself to the level of the "leftovers of creation" as he and his friends were called. David did know that some of his friends had gone with Mr. Mully to MCF in the past and had come back to the street to visit, completely changed. In 1992, David left the street forever. Today he has completed four years of university and is a social worker in Kenya.

Later, on a return visit, I had the unusual opportunity of visiting "Juvenile" as it is called. David was with the small group of people from MCF who went. It was the worst day of my life, before or since.

We drove through the countryside and received gentle instructions from Mully: no cameras, no physical or verbal contact with the children. Basically, we should not do anything that would jeopardize their permission to come into this prison. Outsiders are not allowed in prison, certainly not foreigners. However, there were special circumstances that surrounded this visit. It was the fifteenth anniversary of the Mully Children's Family Home. So many children at the Home had come from this particular juvenile prison that the Mully's wanted to "bless" the prison and the guards and the chil-

> Imagine an orphanage cooking all day to prepare food to take to children in prison.

dren with food and music and ministry to celebrate the fifteen years. It was beyond surreal.

We cooked all day to bring food to the children who often go days without any in this state-run institution. Imagine an orphanage cooking all day to prepare food to take to children in prison. By this point I had read Matthew 25 in the Bible where Jesus talks about bringing food to the hungry and visiting the sick and bringing clothes to people with none and visiting people in prison. I could do that. But I had also read James 1:27. That passage says that we must "look after orphans and widows in distress." My brain cramped up. We had orphans going to visit the people in prison. That is not what is supposed to happen. Why are the orphans going? Why are they preparing the food? This is not what those verses mean. But that is what I saw that day. If I hadn't seen it with my own eyes, I would not have believed it and would not have been able to write it today.

I walked into a concrete building that had a small center court that was no more than six yards by twenty yards long. The prison officials knew that we were coming, so the yard had been swept clean. Even the children were as clean as they had ever been. We were shocked when we heard this because many of them did not have buttons keeping their uniforms closed or zippers keeping their pants closed. None of them had a warm sweater or a long-sleeved shirt to keep them warm, as the African sun dropped from the sky and the temperature dropped to 15°C/60°F. (I couldn't breathe.) It was cold. We spent two hours sitting fifteen feet from the children, a prison rule. David and his MCF friends shared testimony of how they used to be in this very prison and how God had saved them, transformed them, and gave them hope. They played the guitar, sang songs, and danced for the prisoners.

The youngest could not have been more than five years old. (I couldn't breathe.) At the end of the performance it was dark, and we had a short period of time to bring in the food to feed the children. The prison guards and their families were first in line. (I couldn't breathe.) As I picked up a tin bowl that had been badly beaten up, it almost slipped out of my hand. (I couldn't breathe.) They don't wash the dishes, but rather rinse them in cold water, so there were remnants of many meals on each bowl, buried in the crevasses that had been created by the beatings.

Each child was given a huge bowl of vegetable stew (enough for three adults in America) with the meat put in separately to ensure that each one got some. Then each bowl was laden with two giant pieces of chapatti bread. As we handed bowls to the individual children, we tried desperately to touch their hands under the bowl and make eye contact so that we could communicate that we loved them.

As the children went away to sit and eat, I stepped aside from the group and asked David to step with me. The sun had dropped. It was dark. It was cold. I was shaking, but not from the cold. I asked David to share with me his memories from when he was a child in that prison. We stood together, both looking in the same direction toward the wall. I saw a wall; he saw his past. He spoke quietly and slowly as if he were seeing each word come to life in front of him. It was as if he was watching a movie on the wall in front of him and then describing it to me. This is what he said.

> The sun had dropped. It was dark. It was cold. I was shaking, but not from the cold.

"I remember coming here when I was very young. I was a bad boy. The people here are bad people too." He looked briefly over his shoulder and had the eyes of a small child. He continued. "Do you see that man over there? The one who greeted you? He was the worst. I remember him the most."

Then David began to tell me story after story of what life in juvenile prison was like for a child. His sentences were short. The events were short. No need to give too many details. No need to say more than needed saying. But it did need saying. And it may have been the first time that he said it all.

David told me how the head of the prison and the wardens would beat the children and rape them, both boys and girls. He told me how a prison guard who lived nearby would take a girl to his home for the day, and different guards would take turns raping her at the home. In the evening she would be brought back and put in the girls' room. If she had put up too much of a fight, or if they were being particularly sadistic that day, they would throw her into the boys' room. All the girls slept in one room on the floor without mats, mattresses, or blankets. The same was true of the boys' room. Often there would be thirty to forty girls and boys in their respective rooms. The boys' room had a hole in the floor to use as a toilet, but it hadn't been used in a long time. (I can't remember why not.) The result was the boys had been relegated to being animals. Their feces and urine covered the floor of the bathroom and beyond. David told me that there were many days that they would not get food, but on the good days they got one meal, usually consisting of *ugali* (corn/maize porridge). They didn't get meat, and rarely had vegetables added to their meal. They were cold and sick and hungry and in prison, and they were children.

As if I had not heard enough, I asked David what his worst day in Juvenile had been. It was the day a young boy hung himself. When he walked into the boys' room, his friend was hanging and was dead. He thought that maybe the boy was better off. I looked at the children huddled against the wall eating their hot meal and wondered if that were true. I asked David if he thought things had changed here. Is it possible that those atrocities would not be happening to these children, the ones in front of my own eyes? He again looked over his shoulder at the man in charge and said, "No, it is not possible that things have changed. These children should not be here. It is not safe for them. We must pray for them."

As we waited for the door of the prison to be unlocked so that we could leave, I wanted to throw up. I wanted to scream. I wanted to cry. I couldn't look at my team-mates. I looked at the wall and got my final punch in the stomach. There on the wall was a government poster that said, "Say NO to FGM! (Female Genital Mutilation)." My heart ripped open and bled. I was sure I would die of internal bleeding from the pain.

The next morning I awoke to the sound of children singing. There were only a few voices at first, but then more joined in and it sounded like a choir of angels. I got out of bed, splashed water on my face, and followed the voices. I wanted to see what angels looked like. As I stepped out of my tin room, I wasn't sure which way to turn. There were children singing in almost every direction. I randomly chose to go to my left and followed the sound down to the river. There I found one of the many children's choirs practicing their early morning hymns (or whatever it was they were practicing). It was the children's choirs from all over the property that had awakened me with such love. They were singing, their faces were radiant, and their bodies moved to the tune in a way that was magical. How could they do this? How could they sing like this after all they have been through so much? How could they even get out of bed this early if at all?

> They were singing, their faces were radiant, and their bodies moved to the tune in a way that was magical. How could they do this?

I waited until the choir had finished their disciplined time together and walked back with one of the girls. I asked her how she could be so happy, so filled with joy, when she had so little. She looked at me with a big smile and said, "We were singing to Jesus. He is our Father and He is all we need. He gives us joy and we sing to Him." That was my first true glimpse of the transformational power of Jesus Christ.

My first trip to Africa was over. I was going home. Home to my wonderful husband, my beautiful children, my custom-designed house, my BMW, and my big business.

I thought I would die.

Chapter Six

BACK TO LIFE, BACK TO REALITY

The morning after I got back from Africa, I was having coffee in our coffee room at ONYX. I was off in my own world when a few of my office team members came in and started asking questions about my trip. Where could I begin to tell what I had seen? How could I explain the raw situation of life and death in Africa over a cup of java? Water cooler or "coffee talk" doesn't exist where I was in Africa, not just because they don't have water coolers or coffee talk, but because what they talk about is important. I didn't once have a discussion or overhear a conversation with anyone in Zambia or Kenya that wasn't important. Some dialogues were about life and some about death. Some were about food and some water. Some were about their God and some salvation. Some were about their past and some about their future, but none were about nothing. None were gossip or exchanges about the weather. When Africans speak, they have something to say. When they don't have something important or relevant to say, they are silent. Oh, how we could learn that lesson and keep our lives in peace.

So over a seemingly innocent cup of coffee, and an equally innocent question about my trip, the Hopes & Dreams Team was birthed. As I stood talking to Lauri and Rebecca, Steve and Nadine came in and joined the conversation. Within minutes our talk had moved to my next trip. That's right. These young people in my office wanted to join me on my next trip. Next trip? Are they kidding? That *was* my trip.

That was my trip of a lifetime, the one for which I had always longed. It was complete, finished, and besides I didn't think I could ever do something like that again. My heart was broken, bruised, and bleeding. It had changed shape. It no longer had two lovely rounded sides going down into a perky point at the bottom like every Valentine's Day heart. It was now gnarled and torn, never again to be identified as a heart. However, they wanted to go with me.

Another friend, Roberto, one of my senior graphic designers who had been with me at ONYX for ten years, came into the kitchen. He was one of the few Christians in our office and had a real heart for children as well as a compassion for people that was extraordinary. He joined the conversation and immediately said he wanted to go too. Great. I had been out of Africa for forty-eight hours and now had five people from my own office wanting to go to Africa with me on my "next trip." What did that mean?

God? Are you there? What does this mean? Translation please? Apparently I would be leading a team back to Africa.

And so we began. One step at a time. Don't look up, don't look ahead, and don't look behind, just one step at a time. By 5:00 P.M. that day Roberto and Steve (also from the creative department) had already designed a logo for the Hopes & Dreams Team. It was beautiful! We were officially a team. Now all we needed was T-shirts. You have to have T-shirts.

Within a week the Hopes & Dreams Team was rolling. We had business cards, T-shirts, banners, a series of four postcards with information on MCF, and most importantly, we had a plan. The plan included a team of six of us traveling to Kenya in October of 2003. We wanted to raise $25,000 to take back to Kenya to buy a piece of land where we could build a huge playground. There the little ones at Eldoret could have fun and be safe. Each person had to raise their

> We wanted to raise $25,000 to take back to Kenya to buy a piece of land where we could build a huge playground.

own funds to fly to Kenya. To do so, they sold chocolate bars, they held bake sales, and outside barbeques, raffles, etc. All of this fund-raising included our whole office tower, clients, family, and friends. Everyone got involved in helping raise the funds for these young people to go on a trip of a lifetime. I had travel points. Thank you, God, for travel points that had never been used.

The fund-raising for the land and playground hit the tracks fast. I was sitting with my lawyer and dear friend, Ralph, only days after my return. He was playing a weekly game of golf with Ian. We were at the nineteenth hole watching the other golfers finish up their games as I poured my heart out to him about what I had seen. I felt alive and yet dead in a strange way. Here I was sitting at one of the top golf courses in Ontario, where my husband was a member, sipping on a cold Stella Artois and telling my high-priced lawyer (sorry, Ralph) about the nine-year-old girls who were prostituting themselves on a daily basis just so that they could get a piece of bread. These girls were not girls I had only read about in our national newspaper or had seen on Oprah. I had met these girls. I had spoken with these girls. I had looked into their eyes and saw their pain and their shame. These girls were ashamed of their past life (over which they had very little, if any, control) and they lived in that shame until they were freed of it. Freedom is often found by talking about it, sharing it with others, counsel, and prayer.

I told Ralph about one little girl named Elizabeth whom I had met in Kenya. I had been told that she ran away from home to live on the streets when she was only six years old.

Common sense (and having a six year old at home) told me that this couldn't be right. She was a teenager now and had lived a terrible life until she had been rescued by MCF. I asked if I could interview her and find out what had really happened. As a part of their healing, the children are encouraged to speak of their past in safe environments. Elizabeth sat and began to tell me her story.

When she was a little girl both her mother and father beat her. This is very common in Africa, and every child expects to be beaten. Not spanked, but beaten, for any and all offences. Beatings happen to someone in the house on a daily basis and when they commence, all who are not in that immediate beating, scatter to the corners of the hut to escape. African children are beaten with sticks, whips, pots, wire, or anything else that is close at hand. Elizabeth was used to the beatings and expected them. She was also used to her father having sex with her. This had been happening with great regularity for a couple of years before her sixth birthday. Again, this is not an uncommon occurrence on the continent of Africa. What could she do? Her mom had to know. The hut where she lived was tiny, and the land fairly sparse. It couldn't have been a secret. But, in fact, in many cases the mothers in Africa welcome their daughters getting to an age that their husband can have sex with the girl, as it takes pressures off the mother and lessens her chance of getting pregnant again or contracting another sexually transmitted disease. It was the girl's unspoken duty. And besides, she is young. She will forget. Life is hard in Africa. The earlier she learns that, the better.

Elizabeth withstood the beatings and the rape day after day. Many days, there was no food in the house, and those were the hardest days to endure the torture. At least with a full belly she could escape in her mind to her favorite tree, but with no food in three days, the forced sex was unbearable. One day when Elizabeth's mother was out, her father came to her again, but this time it was different. This time he brought her older brother with him. Together they raped her six-year-old body. When they were finished, she cleaned up and walked out. Life on the street had to be better than this. She walked out of her village, left her life behind, and headed towards Eldoret where she would find a new family who would feed her and care for her and maybe even love her. She would take her chances. It had to be better than home. Sadly, she quickly found out, it was not.

Ralph sat in stunned silence. He wasn't looking at me or at the green or at his Stella Artois. He just looked. He was empty. There was a long silence, and then there was more silence. Then he asked his practical lawyer question, "What are you going to do?" I told him about raising $25,000 and building a playground.

He said, "Put me in for five." Put him in for five? What did that mean? Five what? I too, was stunned.

"Five thousand," he said. Our fund-raising had begun, and my casual conversations over coffee at golf or at dinner parties had changed forever.

The Hopes & Dreams Team worked like crazy. They did their day jobs *and* raised money for their own travel *and* worked on initiatives to raise the funds for the playground. The rest of ONYX got involved too, from sponsoring children on a monthly basis from MCF to asking clients to support us with silent auction items for our big fund-raising evening. The production/purchasing department had a special homemade

Italian lunch in our photo studio for outside suppliers and raised almost $10,000. Everyone helped with a backyard silent auction at our home in August where we raised an additional $24,000. We were blessed. The work was getting done and the money was pouring in. With the extra funds raised we could now build a medical clinic on site as well as install boys' and girls' pit latrines, teeter-totters, swings, monkey bars, and a soccer pitch. It was amazing.

> We were blessed. The work was getting done and the money was pouring in.

The day before the backyard auction, I received an e-mail from a woman named Kelly whose daughter was in the same class as our son, Spencer. She worked at a Christian book distributor and said she had just read the manuscript of Dr. Bruce Wilkinson's new book called *The Dream Giver*. She e-mailed his manuscript to me, telling me to read it right away . . . today . . . starting with the last chapter. I explained that I had a large fund-raiser the next day and she replied, "It doesn't matter. You have to read this today! The book was written for you!" So, in my highly-developed way of delegating tasks, I forwarded the e-mail to my trusted assistant, Pam. I asked her to print it and read it "*today*" and give me the gist. Pam is not a big reader, so for her to have to plow through this book for me was an unfair request. However, the next day Pam arrived at my house, where the gals were all dicing and slicing in preparation for the big party, and handed me the manuscript saying, "You have to read this today. It was written for you!"

The party was a success. People sobbed as I shared the real stories and pictures of what was happening to the children and cheered when donations were announced! While the steel drums were played by the pool (sadly playing the 70s ballad of "Feelings" at one point), and the cold, donated champagne was passed, our guests bid on the auction items. The night was perfect. The next day I sat down to read the book that apparently had been written for me. As instructed, I started at the last chapter.

The Dream Giver, written by Dr. Bruce Wilkinson, is a story about a man named "Ordinary" who lived in the "Land of Familiar." The book is a gentle wake-up call to all of us who have a big dream to do something bigger than ourselves, but maybe that dream has been squashed by fear, friends, or family. The story follows Ordinary through his journey to find purpose in his life and allows us to share in his battles with fear, "border bullies," and silence. The final chapter is a personal explanation from Dr. Wilkinson on how *The Dream Giver* applied personally to his life. This author had just moved to South Africa with his family, because he heard God calling them there. He had packed up his house in Atlanta, left the company that he had been with for twenty-five years (in fact, had founded), and moved to Africa. Hey! That is what I wanted to do, but I am still in Canada. How did he do it? What would he do in Africa? How could I get involved? This was perfect.

So I then became a stalker (or so my husband called me). I had to meet Dr. Bruce Wilkinson. I had connections in high places (or so I thought), so was confident that I could hunt him down. However, he had just moved to Johannesburg, South Africa, from Atlanta, Georgia, and the usual sources did not have his forwarding address. To put it a different way, he hadn't really landed yet. That wasn't good enough for me, so I started sending e-mails out to any and all whom I thought might hear from him. And then I waited. And I waited. Nothing happened. This great author who wrote this book for *me* would never know that he had written it for me. What a shame.

> This great author who wrote this book for *me* would never know that he had written it for me. What a shame.

Well, back to work. And back to Africa. The Hopes & Dreams Team continued to raise money as well as collect goods to take with us including thousands of dollars of medical supplies, handmade blankets, school supplies, and new clothes. A few days after the silent auction, a man called and asked if the children could use shoes. He had seen a picture in my presentation of the badly torn shoes that children wore and was moved by it. We gratefully accepted his offer, and within days, we had 100 brand new pairs of shoes!

The team got their many shots, loaded up on malaria pills, and we were off to Africa in October 2003. This was a trip that no one would ever forget—not even the Africans.

Now, you may be asking, "Janine, what about your day job? How did you run this big company while doing all this for Africa?" The truthful answer is that I didn't do it well. I couldn't focus on the things of the past. I would be called into "important" business meetings to discuss the dip in sales of one of our favorite breakfast cereals or our favorite candy bar. These issues would be referred to as "crisis meetings,"

and our clients needed all hands on deck to move their business forward. All I could see were the faces of the children in Africa. I couldn't focus, I lost interest, and I was doomed. My business was doomed, unless God himself stepped in to stop its demise.

Chapter Seven

LILLIAN

The team had an uneventful flight to Kenya (always a good thing) and followed my original trail back up to Eldoret and then on into the Kipsongo slum again. I had told my Africa stories to many people and had shown my photos dozens of times, but there was a part of me that didn't believe it had actually happened. Had I really seen what I saw in April? Was it possible? I had to go back and "see for myself" again . . . and it was almost as if it was the first time.

As we drove into Kitale the smell wasn't as bad as I had remembered; it was the dry season this time. But when we got to the entrance, it all flooded to the front of my brain. I had been here before. I had seen the homes made of garbage. It had been real . . . and it still was real. We walked through the homes, down the paths, and visited with the sick and the elderly. Mully shared with the people about how much Jesus loved them, and they all joined in song to celebrate the day that the Lord had made. Again, they had nothing but joy.

> I couldn't imagine how you could identify one child as more desperate than another in this place.

Just after we entered the area, a man came over to us and told Mully that there was a very desperate child we must see. I couldn't imagine how you could identify one child as more desperate than another in this place. There were children everywhere, many of them with little or no clothing; most had never had a bath. They were starving, bloated, and had ringworm and infections. Every opening in their bodies was leaking something, and yet there was a "desperate child"? Mully continued on with his work and told the man that he would speak with him later. I wasn't sure if the man was drunk or high on brewe or just a bit "off," but he was persistent if nothing else. He kept tugging on Mully's sleeve and then mine and anyone else's who was with our group. As we were at the end of our visit, the man pleaded one more time for us to see the child. This man, accompanied by a large group of villagers, led us to a hut just like the others. We were told that the desperate case was inside. I wasn't sure what to expect. I knew my husband wasn't terribly thrilled that I was back in Kenya, and he certainly wouldn't be thrilled that I was crawling into a small pile of garbage, in the dark (there are no windows or natural light inside) to see a desperate child. I decided I should take a photo as I went it so just in case I was attacked, at least they would know who got me.

I crouched down and crawled into this little hut. It took a minute for my eyes to adjust. As I pushed the button on my camera, the flash illuminated the space for a brief moment. My eyes must have deceived me. I could have sworn that I saw a naked skeleton sitting there looking at me. My eyes adjusted and Mully moved closer to the being that was in front of us. And there she was. Lillian.

Lillian sat wrapped in an old piece of burlap. She was a skeleton. A living skeleton. We could see this because she was completely naked. We learned that her parents had died approximately eight months prior to us arriving, most likely from AIDS. Lillian was near death; you didn't have to be a medical professional to know that. She was dying right in front of our eyes. Her eyes were as white as snow as her head turned from one voice to the next. This snowy look was from anemia. We later found out that she was blind from malnutrition.

Lillian took my breath away. Mully spoke softly to her and asked what her name was and how she was doing. She was too weak to speak and only a tiny, dry squeak of a cry came out of her. Mully immediately said, "We must pray for her right now. He knew how serious it was. He raised his hand and began to pray in and out of Swahili and English. He asked for complete healing of her body and that the Lord would have mercy on her life and bring her back from the brink of death. When he was finished, he spoke to the elders and acquired the proper permission to take Lillian with us to the hospital.

One of the local women came in and tried to put a piece of clothing over Lillian to cover her, but we realized as she tried to put Lillian's arms through the sleeves that her arms would not straighten. Her arms and legs had atrophied into the position she had been in—arms wrapped around her knees to keep warm. They would not straighten. Her legs were covered in what looked like caked-on dirt. We later discovered that this was scurvy (vitamin C deficiency). The woman managed to get Lillian covered up in spite of her cries. She was in pain, she was afraid, and she was dying. As she was carried out of the hut, Mully announced to the community of onlookers that he would be taking her to the hospital in Eldoret and would care for her at the Mully Children's Family Home. We hurried off.

The two-hour drive on wretched roads seemed to take days. The plan was that we would go directly to see Dr. Jumbi, the long-time family doctor of the Mully's children. This doctor is so amazing and kind to the home that they have often driven six hours from Ndalani to Eldoret just to have the children see Dr. Jumbi. We finally arrived with Lillian crying almost the whole way in the arms of another street child who was also rescued. Neither girl had ever ridden in a car before, and we were likely the first white people Lillian had seen.

When we arrived at Dr. Jumbi's office, we prayed over Lillian again, and then sat speechless as we waited to see him. He saw us within minutes. With permission, our team member, Stephen, video-taped the examination. Dr. Jumbi unwrapped her so that he could see what was under the cloth, and Lillian's true status was revealed. He examined her as if she was a rare and unusual bird. He spoke to the camera and showed us her anemic eyes, her paper-thin skin, her malnourished arms and legs, her atrophied joints.

Then he turned her so that we could see every bone in her spinal column. The skeleton. He tipped her forward and pulled back the cloth to reveal her hip bone and the raw, bleeding skin that he called pressure sores where her own weight of sitting without movement had caused the skin to rupture. Her hair was almost gone and what hair she did have was an orangey-yellow color, again from malnutrition. Lillian had a terrible cough; one that Dr. Jumbi said was mostly likely tuberculosis.

As he examined her, he listened to the minimal family history that Mully had been given by the village people. He then continued to say that she could very possibly have AIDS (as both parents were young, died in a close time frame to each other, and it was thought that they were HIV positive) and likely had malaria and typhoid. There was a pause in the diagnosis, and I took the opportunity to ask Dr. Jumbi what the odor was that was a coming from Lillian. It was not like anything I had ever smelled or hope to ever smell again. He looked at me and calmly said, "That is what we call the smell of death. Her internal organs are starting to disintegrate and she only has about twelve hours to live. If you had gone to Kipsongo tomorrow instead of today, you would have found Lillian dead."

We were stunned. He went on to say that she still may not live. It was very likely too late. She had two types of malnutrition. We had to get her to the hospital immediately. We got in the van and drove directly to the hospital.

> She was crying and mumbling that she wanted to go home. Home? She wanted to go home? Back to hell?

Mully went to the office to register the child. I went looking around the children's ward. It was empty. There was only one other child in the entire ward.

How could this be? The slum was full of sick children. The roadsides were lined with children who looked as if they should be in the hospital. But the beds were empty. I asked Mully's son Kaleli why there were no children there. He explained that no one could possibly afford the ten dollars per day that it would cost to come to this private hospital.

After some time Mully came back and Lillian was brought to a crisp, white, clean bed. The young girl who carried her took the dirty rags off her and wiped her with them to remove the feces that was covering her lower body. She was so tiny lying in that big bed, and she was absolutely terrified. She was crying and mumbling that she wanted to go home. Home? She wanted to go home? Back to hell? Back to a place where no one cares for you after your parents die? Back to being alone in the

> I couldn't believe it.

dark? Back to being hungry and thirsty and naked and dying? I couldn't believe it. Mully and Kaleli tried to comfort her, but she just cried.

When I got home that night I wrote in my journal about the day. I recorded that we had found a young child who was approximately two years old. We later found out that Lillian was eight years old and weighed twelve pounds when she arrived at the hospital.

A nurse or two came by to look at the "creature." None really wanted to touch her, but merely to see what had been brought in. Only the wealthy brought their children to this hospital.

A nurse finally came along to take blood so that we could see exactly what diseases Lillian had. We prayed for her again (actually we prayed continuously from the moment we met her). The nurse was unable to get any blood as her veins had collapsed. They had to call a doctor to help. After a very long wait, the doctor arrived to take blood. He walked into the ward and put on a pair of gloves. He then came around to the side of the bed where he could see her tiny face. He paused and went back and put on a second pair of gloves.

Again he came to the side of the bed and pulled back the covers to reveal her skeletal frame. He paused, pulled the sheets back up again, removed his gloves and said, "I am not touching this child," and walked away. He walked away! He never came back. We never saw him again. He refused to help this child.

If I had an ounce of emotional strength left, I would have jumped on his back and beaten him to the ground. But I didn't. I just stood in stunned silence. I was watching another horror film. Mully didn't flinch. He pulled out his cell phone and called Dr. Jumbi at his office to tell him what had happened. Within an hour Dr. Jumbi came to the hospital and took blood from Lillian in the only place that he could—the jugular vein in her neck. We again stood in stunned silence and watched.

We decided to go home and eat, shower, and then come back for the test results. I have no recollection of the rest of the evening, but do remember getting the news. A doctor called with the impossible. Blood tests revealed that Lillian had no tuberculosis (even her cough was gone), no typhoid, no malaria, and NO AIDS! It was a miracle. Impossible. Our God is the God of the impossible, and He showed His greatness that day. The doctor could not believe the results, but did say that he had seen miracles happen before when Mully prayed, so he wasn't surprised.

That night we went back to see Lillian and took Rahab with us to stay with her, comfort her, and insure that she was cared for. Rahab is a young woman who was raped at the age of nine. When she told her mother what had happened, she called Rahab "damaged goods" because she could no longer demand a dowry from a future husband's family. Because Rahab was of no value anymore, her mother threw her out of the house. She lived on the streets as a prostitute from that day until she was rescued by the Mully's at age twelve. Like many of the girls, she ran back to the streets several times over the next ten years and suffered the effects of sexually transmitted diseases, beatings, rapes, and HIV.

It may seem crazy to us, but the freedom and drugs and sex on the streets lure many girls back time and time again. When I first met Rahab in April, she was at death's door. She had full-blown AIDS and was too weak to walk. She too was a skeleton and couldn't have weighed more than sixty pounds. A week after we left, the Mully's received the money needed to purchase lifesaving anti-retro viral drugs for Rahab. She was feeling much better by the time we saw her in October. In fact, her recovery was nothing short of miraculous. She had put on weight, was active, and was back in school and living a reasonably normal life. It was she who came and slept with Lillian that night to comfort and love her. I wept.

Lillian stayed in the hospital for the next three-and-a-half months. We were told that with such advanced malnutrition, she could still die. We knew that would not happen. Our team committed to raising the funds needed for Lillian's hospital stay. When the Mully's went to pick her up, we were able to transfer the funds to them to pay her $4,000 hospital bill (thanks to people who donated to 100 Huntley Street when they aired the Lillian footage).

When I went back to MCF in July, 2004, I could not believe my eyes. There was Lillian, the most beautiful little girl I had ever seen. She was alive. She was a child of God. She had been chosen. She was one child. She was worth the trip to Kenya and I would do it again in a heartbeat.

During that same trip in July, 2004, and on a subsequent trip in April, 2005, we found out that Lillian had two older sisters. Both had been sent away by the village elders after their parents had died. They were told that Lillian was too sick and she would die, but they could live by going to the streets. So, at the age of nine and ten these two sisters were on their own, doing the unimaginable to survive. We were able to find one sister on each of the two visits to Kipsongo over the eighteen-month period since Lillian was found.

The older sisters both thought that Lillian had died. You can't imagine the look on their faces when we brought them to the home in Eldoret and they saw each other for the first time. I know that the angels sang at that moment, I heard them. There was rejoicing in heaven and on earth that day. Those were three of the best days of my life. Lillian and her two sisters are alive and thriving at the Mully Children's Family Home today. I think of them and pray for them often and can't wait to see what purpose God has for each of them.

Although the rest of the trip was amazing, it seemed to pale in comparison to the experience with Lillian. We visited the children in each home again and delivered the many large bags of shoes, socks, vitamins, and underwear that had been donated to us for the children. I felt as if I was at home. I was comfortable and welcome and not judged for what I had or did not have, did or did not do. What a difference from home where we all judge each other by how fast we are running the race and who is winning. Remember the slogan, "He who dies with the most toys, wins"? That didn't seem to apply at the Mully Children's Family Home.

> I felt as if I was at home. I was comfortable and welcome and not judged for what I had or did not have, did or did not do.

We finished the trip by climbing the magnificent mountain that overlooked Mully's 150 acres and the winding Thika River. The boys that took karate lessons at MCF often jogged the mountain for training, and although I had no desire or ability to jog, I was certain that I could at least climb it. Now (hindsight being 20/20) I really am unsure why I thought I could climb it. I was turning forty in a couple of weeks. I had not exercised in a couple of years and I hadn't truly been in shape in for a couple of decades. What was I thinking? I was thinking, *If these young'uns can do it, so can I!* The pride of an almost middle-aged woman, who was used to doing anything that she put her mind to, got to me. So off we went at 5:30 A.M. so that we could be close to summiting when the sun rose.

The hour-long journey took us two hours and my friend Lauri and I were sucking wind pretty badly by the time we reached the top. It was very rocky as there was no natural path. We even left the goats behind somewhere near the middle of the climb. When we reached the top, we were overwhelmed with the beauty of the plain below. We could see for many miles and it was all brown and dry, with the exception of 150 acres of land that was watered by hand and with minimal irrigation systems at MCF. We sat quietly with the kids who had climbed with us, most of them the very children who had shared their life stories with me earlier in the year. We sang a Zulu song that said, "We are marching in the light of God." We truly were.

It was time for us to head back down and continue with our work. It was very hot, we had no food or water, but I was almost forty and feeling great. The pitch was steep and it was very rocky, so I started to hop like a goat from stone to stone, picking up momentum with each leap. After twenty successful hops, I had a less successful connection between foot and rock. I heard a distinct "crack" over the silence of the mountain and found myself sitting on a rock, in the middle of my descent, in pain with a broken leg. Both my tibia and fibula were broken, and I had torn all the liga-ments* around my right ankle. And here I was in the middle of Kenya in East Africa a million miles from home.

My acute pain and the realization that I couldn't call a medical helicopter to evacuate me, brought tears to my eyes before my mind knew I was in trouble. With Stephen and

---

* Common treatment for a sprained ankle or torn ligaments in rural Africa is to use boiling hot water while massaging the damaged area. There was not a piece of ice for 100 miles. I was awakened by this lov-ing treatment (!) after I got back to my room and passed out from stress, exhaustion, and pain.

Roberto by my side, I painfully hopped on one foot and slid on my bum down the rest of the mountain. We were met at the bottom by Peter Mully and his pickup truck. I had never thought of being thankful to God for drought, but if the river had not been dry, Peter would not have been able to get there to save me. I was convinced that I could have died on that mountain and been eaten by goats. (I later came to my senses and realized that goats are herbivores).

After spending a night being heavily self-medicated, I was driven to Nairobi where we went to the Agha Khan Hospital to be officially treated. No more boiling water. They did not put a cast on my foot as I was about to go on a thirty-hour trip to North America, so they wrapped it in gauze and sent me on my way. From the hospital I was driven to the airport to fly home to Toronto, Canada, via Florida. That's right. I was leaving the Mully Children's Family Home filled with hundreds of street children and "criminals," to fly to West Palm Beach and stay at the Breakers Hotel for a global marketing agency bi-annual conference. Having lived on the farm in Ndalani for the prior week, I wasn't terribly clean. I had a broken leg (wrapped in really dirty gauze from my global travel) and was wearing the cleanest of my dirty clothes.

When I landed, Ian was there to meet me. I was a sight (and had a smell) that only a husband could love. Two hours after arriving I was at a black tie dinner in a wheelchair. Even though I was dirty, and tired, and in pain when I arrived, the worst part of all was that I had left my heart in Kenya with my other "family." I now felt that I was entering a foreign land—a land of luxury and emptiness and loneliness. It was as if I had never been here before, but I had. For thirteen years I had made lots of money, traveled the world, stayed at the nicest hotels, ate in the finest restaurants, and drove the nicest cars. I had lived in luxury and emptiness and loneliness, but didn't even know it. However, when I was pushed in my fancy wheelchair to that black tie event in November, 2003, I knew my life as I had known it, was over. I had changed and my life would be different forever.

Chapter Eight

MY GOLDEN CALF

During this time of searching, I was watching a Christian television preacher one Sunday morning as I was preparing to go to church. It was Charles Price, who I believe is a very good teacher from the People's Church in Toronto. He was speaking about Moses and the Israelites who had been freed from Egypt and were traveling through the desert for 40 years. I had heard the story dozens, if not hundreds, of times in my life. I always scoffed at those silly, undisciplined people who had enough belief in God to be led out of slavery and into the desert, but couldn't wait forty days for Moses to come down the mountain with further instructions from the very God they believed led them there in the first place. Instead they started to build a golden calf—an idol to worship. They couldn't keep their eye on God for more than a month before looking elsewhere. What was wrong with them?

I understand that hindsight is 20/20, and I am looking at the story from the end of it, but come on, guys, forty days and you have changed gods? That's a pretty big decision to make on the fly. Each time I heard a sermon about this silliness, I dismissed the people as a weak, undisciplined nation who really lacked any real faith at all. Then Charles Price said it. He stated, "Of course today we do not build golden calves or switch from Christianity to Hinduism in short order, but we *do* worship other gods." What? I certainly don't worship other gods. Who was he speaking to? Then he went on to explain one of the simplest truths I had ever heard, I felt really stupid for missing it for the first forty years of my life. (I guess that's why we hear the same story dozens or hundreds of times.)

The simple truth was that *anything* that we put before our God is a god we worship. We, as Christians, are to have no higher priority than God. God first, family second. Then he tossed out a simple little statement that broke through the screen of the television suspended in my bathroom. He said, "Some people put their work before God. They spend more time thinking about work, driving to work, doing work than they spending thinking about, being with, or talking to God." He went on to speak of children and other things being put first, but my world had just been flipped upside down.

> My golden calf's name was ONYX. I had built it, polished it, spent time with it, worshiped it, and decorated it with beautiful things. But most importantly, I put it *way* ahead of my God . . . and sadly, my family.

Is it truly possible that I was so blind for almost forty years? Interestingly, that is the same number of years the Israelites wandered in the desert with Moses. Is it possible that I missed this simple truth, and that I, too, had a golden calf? Yes, I had a golden calf for fifteen years. My golden calf's name was ONYX. I had built it, polished it, spent time with it, worshiped it, and decorated it with beautiful things. But most importantly, I put it *way* ahead of my God . . . and sadly, my family. I was a stupid Israelite with no self-discipline or sense. I almost dropped to the floor. "Thou shalt have no other gods before me" rang through my ears. I was breaking one of the Big ten! This had to change!

In November, 2003, I officially hit the age forty, and as Christmas quickly approached, I simply couldn't get in the spirit of the season. I had just returned from my second trip to Africa, just come back from helping rescue Lillian and was really beginning to understand the depth and breadth of the crisis in Africa. How could I decorate my house with hundreds of lights and silly Santa figurines? I wasn't prepared to bake endlessly to give people more food than they already had so that they could put on that extra ten pounds that they do every year. I couldn't go out and shop tirelessly for gifts that people didn't need or want. Children in Africa were starving. Children there have no clothes. How can I sit and pretend that I didn't see that? How can my life go on? How do I process what I know to be true with the life that I am living? After all, I have children who aren't hungry, who have closets full of clothes, and who are expecting a mound of presents under the tree.

I was nauseous at the thought of preparing a huge meal on Christmas day and eating until we couldn't eat anymore. Across my street, my city, and my country this would be happening while meanwhile, on the other side of the world, people would be picking through another garbage bin and hoping to get something to eat that wasn't too rotten. There would be no turkey, stuffing, vegetables, cookies, or Christmas pudding, which I made every year even though no one really liked it, but it was tradition. Tradition had to change. The madness had to stop. I couldn't do it anymore. I would have a breakdown. I had to leave. My head was spinning. My mind wouldn't stop.

So our family didn't decorate. We didn't bake nor did we prepare a Christmas meal. We spent very little on Christmas gifts for our friends and family. Instead, we went to Mexico.

We spent two weeks on the beach enjoying the sun and surf. Now, you might be thinking, *Oh that was a big sacrifice, Janine. The children in Africa don't get to go on holiday to the beach either.* But it was what I did. I had to break the Christmas traditions of the past, and hope that some would be forgotten in a year (our children were still small, so it was possible), and then new traditions could be created the following Christmas. We had a $50 maximum on the gifts to each child and to each other. When Christmas morning came, these few small gifts were found under a construction paper Christmas palm tree that the children had made and taped to the coffee table. It was perfect. It was small. It was short. Then we went to the beach.

On the way there, I sensed that I should go to the business office and check my e-mail. When I told Ian where I was going, he thought it was a very odd thing for me to do, as I never checked e-mail when I was away on holiday. When we were away, we were truly away. We left work, home, and family behind and tried to remain present wherever we were. So this was unusual for me, but something was telling me to go check. And so I did.

There it was. Christmas morning, an e-mail from Dr. Bruce Wilkinson, saying that he had heard I was trying to reach him. He explained that he was back from Africa (where he had moved with his family) and was in America for the holidays. He would be traveling to various cities to speak for the next month. He asked what it was I wanted to speak to him about and gave me his personal schedule as well as phone numbers so that I could contact him directly. I couldn't believe my eyes. What a Christmas gift! Dr. Bruce Wilkinson, author of squillions of books, had written to me! We were going to meet. I knew it. I didn't know why, but I knew we would. And we did.

Boys sleeping on the street in Zambia

Homes made of garbage in Kenya

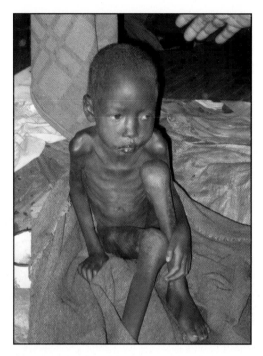

Lillian—8 years old, 12 pounds when rescued

Lillian (middle) and her two sisters—18 months later

Swazi Grandfather used the door to make a coffin

Swazi family receiving blankets and food

Children raising children in Swaziland

Chief Jambulani in Malawi

Just after we got home from Mexico, I flew down to New York City where Dr. Wilkinson had a whole day open in his schedule. We sat and drank coffee and talked for hours at the Waldorf Hotel. I told him how unhappy I was in my business and how much I wanted to pack it all in and move to Africa. After all, he had done it, so why couldn't I? It was a long, tearful day. I laughed and cried as I poured out my heart and shared about my business, my life, my children, and my heart for Africa. At some point during the day Dr. Wilkinson asked me if I was actually running "to" Africa or running "away" from Canada/work/life. I was stunned. I didn't know the answer to that. I was too emotionally confused, medicated, and distraught to answer that question honestly. He suggested I go back to work and focus all my energy on my business for the next ninety days while praying and asking God for direction on what I was to do. I didn't want to focus on ONYX for the next ninety days. I wanted to pack up and run away. But I shook hands on it. I committed to do that and I did it.

For ninety days I gave it my all. My business had been in decline for the past year because my heart wasn't in it. My focus was where my heart was . . . Africa. I wasn't physically, emotionally, or spiritually present at the office. I had checked out. But now I was checking back in and I was going to give it my all—but my all wasn't much. We did amazing new business presentations that blew people away, but we didn't get the business. Business and competition was getting harder every day. We were a big machine that needed a lot of fuel to keep it running. At our peak we had 75 employees and a 18,500 square foot office that cost $45,000 per month just for rent. Our

> My focus was where my heart was . . . Africa.

payroll was in the millions, and our clients were all blue chip companies. We were the Canadian Agency of Record for great companies like Disney, Kellogg Canada, Labatt Breweries, and Gillette Canada. Our clients were awesome and fun to work with. Many people in their leadership became my closest friends over the years. We were a creative and fun and hip and cool company. Our logo was brilliant. Our team was brilliant. Our work was brilliant. We won awards in Canada and globally and were recognized as real industry leaders in our thinking, our creativity, and our approach to breaking through in the market.

For 90 days I worked and created and pitched, and continued to die inside. I was living a lie. I was playing office. I couldn't keep up the façade and people knew it. By April, 2004, only one short year after I first stepped foot in Africa, I was going to work in denim overalls and T-shirts. My Ellen Tracy suits were collecting dust in the closet. The thirty pounds that I put on during these days assured that the designer clothing stayed in the closet. I was finished. I cried out to God and asked Him what I was to do. I cried so much that I stopped wearing make-up to work because I just cried it all off anyway. People didn't know what to think of me. Had I snapped?

On April twenty-eighth, my girlfriends, Maureen and Vikki, were in the office on official Hopes & Dreams Team business. I was an emotional mess. They asked if I wanted to pray. I said okay. We went to the back corner of the office so that no one would see us. As we sat in this empty office for thirty minutes, they prayed and I cried. They asked God to give me an answer as to what I was to do and asked Him to specifically give me a sign. A sign? What kind of sign would God give *me*, and would I even recognize it? I cried. At the end both women were overwhelmed with what they said was the Holy Spirit in the room. I didn't feel a thing. How was it that I was the one with the problem, I am the one crying out to God, but they are the ones that feel the Holy Spirit? I was ripped off. What's up with that? Come on, God, what are you doing?

After they left, I got up and went to my office to meet with Garth, my VP of Brand Strategy and Development and my friend, to review the strategic plan for ONYX to move forward. Garth and I had worked together from the first day I started ONYX, even before it had its name. We worked together well. Garth came in and did what I assume was one of his brilliant presentations, but it sounded like he was speaking gibberish. I couldn't understand him. It was as if he was speaking a different language, and I couldn't understand his words. At first I thought that he was having a stroke, but then I thought it must be *me* who was having the stroke. I shook my head. Wiped my eyes and refocused. But no, he was still speaking gibberish. I stood up, looked at Garth, and told him I had to go.

I had a lunch meeting with Ian and Lauri. We had decisions to make. Our office lease was up on July 31, and we had to decide if we were to rent again or buy a building and generally what was going to happen as I continued to spiral downward. No one knew what to do, and everyone was looking to me, as leader and president, for direction. I had none. I was lost. I was empty. I was finished.

> I was lost. I was empty. I was finished.

I went to lunch and as I slid into the booth across from them, I had my answer. I *knew* what God was telling me to do. I looked at them both and started to cry again. I told them that I had to leave ONYX. Lauri looked at me and said, "I know you do." It was over. I had owned ONYX for sixteen years, and it was all over. They asked what would happen with the company, the people, the clients, and I said I didn't know, but I did know that I had to go. I got up and left the restaurant. I just left them there. I went home and cried some more. However, I knew that the decision was right and that it was complete. I knew I had been called to Africa.

When I was young I heard people say in church that they had been "called" to this or "called" to that. I didn't really know what that meant or how someone was "called." I knew that God did the calling, but how? In fact, I was quite certain that I wouldn't know what He sounded like if He did call. I later learned the scripture, "My sheep hear my voice" (John 10:27). When I was in Africa in 2003, only a year earlier, I had heard the call on my life to work in Africa. What I can say with great confidence is that when you are called, you know that it is God who called you. And you know what He is calling you to. Maybe not the specifics, but the call. You just know. And you know that you know. You can't escape it. What you can do is choose to be obedient to the call, or not. My problem wasn't, "Will I?", but rather, "How do I?" fulfill that call. How do I serve Africa when I am serving ONYX? Although I knew what I knew to be true, it didn't make sense. After all, if God gave me a creative mind and a gift for business, then wouldn't it behove Him to allow me to stay in business, prosper my business, and then allow me to give more to His work? That made more sense than for me to leave my business. After all, God needed the cash to feed His people, didn't He? He needed my ability to speak to people and tell them the truth about what is happening in Africa, didn't He? Surely, at the very least, He needed my contact list.

Problem. My husband wasn't called to Africa. In fact, he had no desire whatsoever to even go to Africa. Each time I came back and showed pictures of Kantwa and told Lillian's story, he wanted to go even less. When asked, he would proudly say, "I believe there are goers and senders, and we have been blessed to have one of each in this family." When I pushed him, he agreed to travel to Africa when a Four Seasons Hotel was built there. (One of Ian's goals in life was to stay at every Four Seasons Hotel in the world before he died. He had visited thirteen locations to date).

So how could I be called to Africa and my husband not be even slightly interested? That didn't sound right. When I bounced my concern off some friends, they assured me that God wouldn't call me to something that would separate our family. We may not be called specifically to the same thing, but God doesn't separate families. Although I had to believe them because their logic did sound like God, something inside disagreed because here I was, living proof that God called me to serve people who live in mud huts halfway around the world, while my husband was dreaming of the Four Seasons Hotel in Fiji. I would have to think about this one and have a few chats with God.

> . . . how could I be called to Africa and my husband not be even slightly interested?

We decided to close ONYX. Why not sell it you ask? The answer was, and remains, two-fold. What kept spinning through my head all day and night was that there were fourteen million children who had been orphaned in Africa by the AIDS pandemic. At that time the World Health Organization was predicting forty-three million by the year 2010. Imagine if you can, forty-three million children in sub-Saharan Africa, under the age of fifteen, living alone. The stats spun in my head day and night. If I were to sell ONYX to make more money, I would have to work for three years at the purchasing agency to ensure a smooth transition, profitability, and etcetera. I didn't have three years. Millions of people are dying. Tens of millions of Lillians and Kantwas are being left alone to be raped and beaten and die, and people are wondering why I can't work another three years creating and designing campaigns to help sell more Froot Loops® and Disney DVDs? The people are dying. The children are dying. I had to go. That is the answer I gave my non-Christian friends. For my Christian friends, my answer was simply because that is not what God told me to do. He told me to leave ONYX, and I did. And the next decision was to close it. So we did. It was a train wreck.

I was in a deep depression and headed full on into a nervous breakdown. No one seemed to notice or care. Ian and I were getting all of our family income from ONYX, so what would we do? We had made money and spent money. We had lived large, loved life, and hadn't really put much away. How would we live? And how do you explain to your clients and staff of many years that God told you to close your business of sixteen years? People were angry and confused.

> I was in a deep depression and headed full on into a nervous breakdown. No one seemed to notice or care.

In two short months before our lease expired, we helped almost every one of our staff find new jobs. We made personal and professional recommendations to our clients to work with one of our competitors, and we began to empty the offices. I only made it as far as part one and two. I broke down through part three—emptying the offices. Ian was left to do that, with whomever would volunteer to help. On July 28, I took my third team to Kenya, including our ten-year-old son Spencer, and Ian was left to clean up my mess.

On July 31, the elevators letting people onto our floor were locked. A thirty-foot moving truck filled with everything we couldn't sell, throw away, or give away was brought to our lovely home. We filled all three car bays in our garage as well as our large basement from floor to roof. The ONYX stuff moved in and filled our lives with chaos and clutter.

I was in Africa, following my call when my company of sixteen years died. Ian was in Canada wondering what just happened. God was with us both.

Chapter Nine

THE VALLEY OF THE SHADOW OF DEATH

In 2004 everything around me was dying. It seemed like I had been walking in the valley of the shadow of death for a year. In the months leading up to this, Ian had been rushed to the hospital with a ruptured appendix requiring emergency surgery. Our golden retriever, Murphy, died of cancer after only forty-eight hours of illness. Only weeks after we got our new golden retriever puppy, Sadie, she was sprayed by a rabid bat and had to be put to death. (Rabies can be transmitted through the aerosol spray from a bat's mouth.) This also resulted in a series of forty-eight needles for our whole family as all of us had been sprayed by the bat as well, and would have died had we not been treated within ten days. There is no cure for rabies. Even the plants in our house, in which I used to take great pride, died.

But most importantly, my dad was dying. Dad had been sick for many months and his body was giving out. In fact, he had been sick for most of my life. In 1997 he had a kidney transplant and the years of living with poor kidneys made the rest of his body work much harder than it should have. In the year prior to this time, he had been transferred from one hospital to another where he stayed for months at a time with only short stints at home with my Mom. He did not have cancer or a heart condition, but rather was suffering from old age at the young age of seventy-five. His deteriorating health and worn out body, combined with complications of spinal surgery and some questionable health care, took us through peaks of hope and valleys of despair on a weekly basis and left us in a constant state of asking "Is today the day?"

Sometime in June, Mom decided that he really needed to be at home after many months in a trauma hospital, and so brought him there to be cared for by twenty-four-hour nursing staff. After a week or so, I was awakened early in the morning and felt that I was to go to their house. I did not know why, and was hesitant to go uninvited and unannounced at 5:00 A.M.. When I got there, I found my dad in a delusional state. I was not sure whether he was conscious or not. He looked like a small bag of bones with big eyes. His nurse was sitting beside him calmly reading. I think he recognized me. I knew he was in a critical state.

When their family doctor's office opened, I called him and explained what I had seen. Immediately the doctor called an ambulance, and my dad's frail ninety-pound body was picked up off his bed by the drivers and removed from the house. We all thought that was the last time we would see him alive. I rushed to the hospital and spent the day with him in the emergency room. They kept saying that it did not look good, and that he would likely not last long. We had heard this before, many times. My dad was not only a survivor, but he was afraid to die. My mom was the bigger fighter and wasn't going to let him go. I think her drive to keep him alive was what made him afraid to die. They had been married forty-nine years and together they had cheated death for many months, if not years. At the end of that day, when a room became available in this sleepy little cottage hospital, he was moved upstairs. We were told that he would not likely make it through the night, and we should say our good-byes. I called Ian and he brought our children over to say good-bye to Grandpa, for the last time.

Mom was living with multiple sclerosis and that made her mobility a big challenge. She would use a scooter to travel the one-plus mile to see Dad each day, while still managing a large home and her own health. The stress of my dad's poor health significantly impacted her health, and we could see the strain was taking its toll.

Did I mention I was an only child? Did I mention that I was an adopted child? This interesting combination can easily be translated into the feeling that my parents had put all their eggs in one basket. It's like play craps and betting the farm on one number. I had loved being an only child up until this point. Now I had no one to turn to. Questions were being asked, decisions needed to be made, health issues were in question, and I was on my own.

My business was dead and my father was dying, ...

My business was dead and my father was dying, but "not dead yet" (pardon the Monty Python humor), and I felt like the "walking dead." Dad didn't want to die alone. He suffered from terrible nightmares, so he asked me to stay with him on this night that was sure to be his last. I agreed. Ian took the children home after their tearful good-byes. My mom rode her scooter home in the dark. The wonderful nurses brought me a cot complete with blanket and a pillow to sleep on at the bottom of Dad's bed. I dozed on and off as he tottered between consciousness and unconsciousness for hours.

... and I felt like the "walking dead."

I must have nodded off because the next thing I knew, I was up and out of bed to the screams of my father. His eyes were as wide as saucers, and he was pulling the IV out of his arm. Blood was shooting. He was tearing his skin with his own claw-like nails. He was screaming that we had to kill the chicken. "How do we kill the chicken?" When the nurses ran in to restrain him, he lifted his head off his pillow and in a robotic-like fashion, turned to them and asked without blinking, "Do you know how to kill a chicken?" The nurse told him that she could not. This went on with each nurse until finally a nurse assured him that she knew how to kill a chicken and would take care of it. They cleaned up his wounds, clipped his nails, and gave him something to help him sleep.

He did not die that night or for many months. During these dark days nurses would dial one of my contact numbers from time to time, and I would get these haunting messages on my voice mail from Dad calling out to me. Once he left a message at ONYX on our main switchboard voice mail telling me he was stuck in a box and couldn't get out. He begged and cried for me to come and get him out. Other times he would leave messages on my cell phone, crying for me to come and "spring him" from the hospital. It was awful. I didn't know what to do. I kept the messages and every so often would hear him calling to me, long after his death. I have since erased all but one. I pray that one day I will erase that one too. It haunts me.

Dad spent several months in that hospital and eventually was sent to a nursing home to live. Mom insisted on moving in with him, but left their house intact. She was convinced he would be healed and would move home soon. This was not to be. On January 28, 2005, my dad hit his critical and final stage. He was rushed to the emergency room for the last time. He was unconscious and put on a ventilator. For the next two weeks he was on and off life-support systems of various sorts. He lived in the intensive care unit and was so susceptible to hospital infections that we had to visit him in masks and gowns and that was very upsetting to my disoriented dad who drifted in and out of consciousness. He had twenty-four-hour acute care and was kept as comfortable as possible under the circumstances.

My mom was able to visit him on her scooter and was free to ride around the hospital to get food, coffee, and use the phone to communicate with the rest of the family who was praying that Dad would rally again. He did rally enough to move out of intensive care and back to a normal ward. In the middle of the night on February 13, 2005, we got a phone call from the hospital saying that his breathing had changed and that his time was likely short. I drove to Mom's house to pick her up and we went to see him together. He had an oxygen mask on to help him breathe as it was now impossible for his lungs to get enough air. We sat with him and prayed. Mom sang to him and we talked quietly. At 7:25 A.M. I picked up my Bible and started reading Psalm 23. "Yea, though I walk through the valley of the shadow of death, I will fear no evil for you are with me; your rod and your staff, they comfort me." At 7:30 my dad died. We were there. He was peaceful and comfortable and just slipped off. The moment was bittersweet. Mom was shocked. She really had not expected him to die, probably because he had been at the brink of death so many times before.

I had never been with someone when they died. It was surreal. One minute my dad was there, and the next minute there was just a body. His spirit had left. It was an empty vessel made up of skin and bone and organs. But there was no person there. For a few moments we just stared at him. I took his oxygen mask off and looked at the skin that had pulled taut over his nose from lack of nourishment. The mask straps had left red marks on his skin, but it was just skin, not his skin, because he wasn't there. His eyes were open, but there was nothing behind them. I closed them.

I was obviously in shock, because my mind didn't immediately go to the fact that my dad was gone, but rather that there was a body there.

After my mom and I realized what had happened and we had said our own good-byes, I looked at her and wondered, "What do I do now?" What happens next? There is a body in front of us. Dad is in heaven. What do I do? Do I take him somewhere? How does he get to the funeral home? Is he embalmed here? I went to the nursing station and told them through my tears that he was gone. Even though they knew that the end was near, they, too, seemed shocked by the news. I asked, "What do we do now?" They told me not to worry; they would take care of it. What did that mean? It meant that when we were finished in the room, we just left. They came and covered him up. They sent him down to the morgue. They contacted the funeral home and arranged for the body to be picked up. They would have the funeral home arrange to get Dad's best suit in which he was to be buried. All we had to do is go and pick out the casket and the flowers, arrange the pastor for the service, and call the family. Easy. As painless as possible.

At the same time this was happening, there was a young girl in Africa who also was dealing with a death. Her brother had died. She lived in a small hut in the rural area of Swaziland, near Durban, South Africa. Her brother had been sick for several months too. Each day this young girl would walk several kilometers to get a bucket of water to bring to him, so that he could drink and she could cook him some *pap* (corn/maize flour and water). He had become very, very sick in the past month and would regularly vomit up the food she gave him. He constantly had diarrhea on the mat on which he slept. She would have to clean both him and the mat. He hadn't been able to walk outside to go to the bathroom in the bushes for many weeks. The water she fetched would also be used to clean him and wash the thin blanket she used to cover him. The last two weeks of his life were terrible. He had open sores in his mouth, and they had spread over his lips and cheeks. Often they would bleed. She didn't have anything to put on them and prayed to God that the pain would go away as he cried out in the night.

There was no clinic within walking distance. In fact, she had never laid eyes on a doctor or nurse in her life. Her grandparents were still alive and lived in the house next to her, but they couldn't help. They had eleven other grandchildren living with them because all their parents had died. In the night she would often be awakened from a deep sleep by the terrifying screams from her brother's bed. He was asleep, but was being tortured as he slept. During the last few days of his life, he could not speak or eat or move. He just lay there like a skeleton, with his eyes wide open, staring at the grass roof. Parts of the roof had blown off the winter before in a storm, so the sun would cross his face as the day passed. She sat in the corner of the hut and watched to see him blink. That was all she could do. She had no aspirin or morphine for his intense pain. She couldn't give him food as he couldn't eat anymore.

She knew what was going to happen next. He was going to die. She had seen it before. She had been in a room when someone died. Unlike me, she knew what to expect. And then the expected happened. His shallow breathing slowed

> There was no clinic within walking distance. In fact, she had never laid eyes on a doctor or nurse in her life.

down, he blinked one last time and then there was no more breath. It was over. She didn't have to go over to the mat to see that it was just a body. It was dark anyway as the sun had already passed. His eyes were open, and she would close them when she went to put the blanket over his head. There was no oxygen mask to remove. There was no one to go tell. Her *gogo* (grandmother) told her that today was probably the day that he would die, and Gogo always knew.

She closed her eyes and cried, but there weren't many tears. They were mostly gone. She was all cried out. Over the past three years she had watched as her father died. A few months later her mother died. Within a year, two of her younger siblings died, and now her older brother. There were no more tears. She knew what she had to do. She went and told Gogo and Grandfather that her brother was dead. The sadness in their eyes almost masked their look of hopelessness. There was nothing left to bury him with. Gogo and Grandfather had buried all of their own children—fifteen in total. One by one they all got very thin, had the same thrush in their mouths and on their faces, the same swelling in the neck. Many of them had cancer on their legs or arms that ended up as open wounds oozing on their already soiled clothes. But when her last uncle died, she heard her grandparents say they had nothing left for the burial of anyone else. The look in Grandfather's eyes confused her. It was as if he didn't know what to do. But, of course, he did know what to do. Not only had he dug fifteen holes in the garden to bury his own children, he had dug another seven holes to bury his grandchildren. The next hole would be number twenty-three. What was going through his mind?

She stood and watched as he looked around the yard and then at the house. He went and stood in front of the door of his small home and paused. Then, in one fluid motion, he forcefully removed the door from its hinges, knocking loose some of the mud blocks that were supporting it. She was only puzzled for a moment. She then watched him walk away and knew what he was doing. He was going to make a coffin for her brother. There was no other wood. They were long out of money to buy a coffin. He would make one for his grandson out of his own front door. She stood and watched in stunned silence.

> He was going to make a coffin for her brother. There was no other wood.

My mom was on her scooter as we were guided through the beautiful oak-paneled offices of Low & Low Funeral Home. They led us to a wheelchair elevator that took us downstairs to the showroom for coffins. We had dozens to choose from. None of them cost less than $2,000. They were made from every type of wood: mahogany, teak, oak, and pine. They were lined with satin and cushioned with cotton. Dad's coffin would eventually be placed in a cement box so that it would last longer in the ground without water damage. (I never quite understood that one.) Dad would be embalmed at the funeral home, put in his best blue suit and silk tie, and then my cousin, the funeral director, would do his best to make Dad look as he had looked prior to sickness and death. It was difficult for them because the extreme levels of medication Dad had been on to keep him alive and relatively pain-free, had also changed the texture of his skin. When they applied the makeup (so that friends and relatives could see him . . . dead) his skin tore and caused problems.

Eventually he was prepared for burial. Dozens of magnificent flower arrangements arrived at the funeral home, our home, and my mom's house. Thousands of dollars were donated in lieu of sending flowers to the Russell F. Willis Memorial Children's Library, which was later built in Dad's honor at the Mully Children's Family Home in Kenya. Three days later, friends and family from all over Canada gathered together in a beautiful chapel to remember him and his seventy-seven years of life. Afterward, we gathered in another comfortable room for a lovely spread of sandwiches, cakes, and cookies supplied by the women from my parent's church.

In Swaziland, long after the sun had set, the coffin was finished and had been gently placed inside the hut ready for the body. The body is traditionally wrapped in a blanket and placed in the wooden structure. There was only one blanket left, and it was threadbare, but it would have to do. The girl would be cold at night without a blanket, but she really hadn't shared one with him since he had been sick. Gogo came into the hut and quietly prepared the body for burial. She then asked the girl to help lift him and wrap the blanket around his boney frame. The two of them easily lifted him into the box, and Grandfather pulled back the blanket so that their friends could see his face. A hole had been dug by the neighbors when they saw Grandfather building the box.

The funeral would begin long before the sun came up, and it would be the same as all the other funerals. The women would come into the hut and see the body in the box

> The women would come into the hut and see the body in the box and cry and sing and mourn for hours.

and cry and sing and mourn for hours. When the sun rose, Grandfather would nail the box shut. They would carry it to the garden, to be planted—buried—at the end of the long row. The slow and mournful songs would continue while the box was passed down to the people standing in the hole. The men would then take turns putting shovels full of dirt on top of the coffin. After every five or six inches of dirt were thrown in, a couple of young men would jump on top of the coffin to pack the dirt down tight. This sequence would continue. Sing, shovel dirt, jump. Sing, shovel dirt, jump. When the hole was full to overflowing, the singing would stop, and words would begin. Typically the local chief would give a eulogy about the greatness of the person who had died, their family, and their great lineage. But this time there were few words spoken and few people left to hear them. It was over. The feast that was to follow was small as there was only pap and some mangoes left to eat.

I took my mom back to her empty house where she would now be alone. I tucked my tearful children into bed and then crawled into my own bed and clung to Ian as I wept. How would we go on without Dad?

The young girl found her new sleeping place on the cold mud next to her 11 cousins. There were no blankets left for any of them. They had all been used to wrap dead family members. And now the cold night air was blowing in through the space that once held a door. How would they go on?

Our two families were worlds apart, but we shared the same grief and the same pain. However, our fears could not have been more different. My father lived a good seventy-seven years, and in the end we were blessed to have access to modern medicine, skilled doctors, and the grace of God which kept Dad with us. We were afraid of what life would be like without him. The twenty-three Swazis that died in that one family, died young, uneducated, and without hope for the future. Where was modern medicine to help with their pain? Where were the skilled doctors when they were dying? Where was the grace of God in their lives when they cried out in the night? The ones who were left behind were afraid of what life would be like in the future.

> There were no blankets left for any of them. They had all been used to wrap dead family members.

> *Yea, though I walk through the valley of the shadow of death I will fear no evil for you are with me; your rod and your staff they comfort me.*
>
> —Psalm 23:4

Amen.

Chapter Ten

IS IT OKAY WITH YOU?

So let's back up two weeks, back to January 28, 2005, the day my dad entered the hospital for the last time. Up until that point in the evening my day was nothing short of miraculous.

I had heard through some friends in the publishing world that Dr. Wilkinson was scheduled to come to Toronto for a day to do some filming for the Christian television program 100 Huntley Street. I hadn't see him since we met in New York City a year prior, but I thought he might be interested in the twist of events that had happened since we last met. After all, it was he who suggested that I give ONYX my all for ninety days while praying for God's guidance in my life. I think I sent him an e-mail when we closed ONYX, but I hadn't communicated with him much since then. I had been in contact with his assistant though and I arranged to be the one to greet him at the Toronto airport and take him to his hotel the night before his filming the next day.

I asked Ian if he wanted to come meet this famous author, who happened to have a heart for Africa as I did. Ian declined. He had no interest, but with a small amount of persuasion and the promise of dinner out, Ian finally agreed to join us. We met Dr. Wilkinson at the airport. He quickly became "Bruce" to us, and drove him to his hotel. All the way there, I updated Bruce on what had happened at ONYX, in Kenya, and in our lives. He was fascinated to hear what God was doing. Over dinner Ian became quite intrigued with what Bruce's organization called *Dream for Africa* was doing. At the end of dinner, Bruce encouraged us to come and see him again the next day to continue the conversation at the studio. And so we did. A strange twist of events left Bruce with the next afternoon free as filming was postponed, so we had lunch and ended up talking for five hours. Bruce shared with us the vision that the Lord had given him for *Dream for Africa* in the areas of hunger, orphans, poverty, and AIDS. The vision was huge, but God gave it to the right guy because Bruce embraces and runs with big visions. I would have laughed and cowered in the corner, but not Bruce. He had recruited more than 2,000 people in two years to travel to Africa to help implement this vision. In fact, the first and primary initiative that he was working on was called *Never Ending Gardens*.

The *Never Ending Gardens* program was designed to have volunteers from North America travel to Africa to plant backyard gardens for people who have no food or only cornmeal to eat. It was a ten-day experience that would quickly introduce the volunteers to the truth about what was happening in Africa, while having them stay in a secure hotel with clean water and safe food. The trip participants were able to go into the most remote villages and talk to the people while providing a sustainable food solution for them. They would plant seedlings of cabbage, tomatoes, onions, beets, and other immune-boosting vegetables.

On a continent that sees 30,000 children die every single day due to hunger or malnutrition, this was a first step in helping people feed themselves rather than relying on handouts.

On a continent that sees 30,000 children die every single day due to hunger or malnutrition, this was a first step in helping people feed themselves rather than relying on hand-outs. Many of the homes where they planted the gardens were orphan-headed households. Volunteers would often see nine children living in one hut with no parent to care for them. However, there were reports of twenty-seven to fifty-six children living alone in one hut or being cared for by one grandmother. The children were hungry and most often living on cornmeal flour porridge alone. Those fortunate enough to go to school received their one meal a day at school but nothing else at home. Bruce went on to explain that the next step in this plan was to teach the people how to let some plants go to seed and then harvest the seeds for future planting.

I could see Ian's interest being tweaked. He still wasn't as concerned for the people as he was fascinated by the thought of providing self-sustainable food security through this modular way of thinking. This vision starts small with a ten-foot-square backyard garden, but over time winds up feeding a nation. Ian was interested.

And then the penny dropped. At 5:00 P.M. Bruce asked Ian a simple question. "Why haven't you gone to Africa?" Ian proudly gave his standard "goers and senders" response and smiled. Bruce looked straight into Ian's heart and said, "Now really, why haven't you gone?" Ian paused. There was silence in the room. He then asked Bruce if he had ever seen the pictures I had taken in the slums of Kenya. Had he seen Lillian's picture? Had he seen where Kantwa lived on the street and heard what had happened to him? Ian went on to admit that he didn't think he could handle those situations.

Bruce assured him that he wasn't leading teams of people to see those extreme situations, but rather, his trips were a great introduction to Africa. They were safe, physically *and* emotionally.

Ian laughed nervously and said, "Well, Bruce, I think when I decide to go to Africa, it will most likely be on one of your trips." Ian confidently sat back, sensing he had avoided all danger.

Bruce smiled as only Bruce can and said, "Why don't you come on my next trip?"

Ian asked, "Oh, when is that?"

Bruce chuckled and said, "We leave Sunday morning." It was Friday at 5:00 P.M.

There was silence in the room. Dead silence. Not the kind of silence where you could hear a pin drop, but the kind of silence where you could hear a fly breathe. I personally was holding my breath, but screaming on the inside at the same time. This was it! This was the moment I had been praying for. I looked at Bruce and then looked at Ian and screamed at him at the top of my lungs (in my mind). *SAY YES!!!* And then do you know what happened? Ian said yes. But not two seconds went by before he flippantly said, "Oh, I can't go. I don't have any of my shots. And I know how many shots Janine needed to go to Africa." My heart sank. He was right. And then Ian's words hit Bruce and rebounded from the other side of the table. Bruce looked at Ian and his smile got bigger as he said, "Do you have a valid passport?"

Ian said, "Yes."

Bruce said, "Well, that's all you need. You don't need shots for Swaziland. Will you come with me on Sunday?"

Now a little side note here. Ian is not a "Mr. Jump-First-Look-Later" guy. He is an operations man. Things are well planned, well thought out. *No* jumping first. He looks first, evaluates, plans, second-guesses himself, and revises the plan. Then, and only then, does he act because he is sure what the results will be. And this was Africa we were talking about, not trying a new flavor of Ben and Jerry's ice cream.

There was a long silence, more intense than the first. The room was thick with silence. I was still screaming in my head, and couldn't believe that Bruce didn't look at me and tell me to be quiet as if the sound was leaking out of my ears. And then I had a brief moment thinking, "Hey, what the heck? I'm the Africa chick here and Bruce didn't even glance my way when he extended the invitation to Mr. Non-Africa. What's up with that?" But I sat silently. I literally bit my tongue and had the cognitive thought that if there was *ever* a time for a wife to be still and keep her mouth shut, this was the time. In sales, one of the big rules is that once you ask for the sale, you stay silent. You wait as long as you have to until the person you are trying to sell breaks the silence. I thought Ian was going to throw up. I didn't know what was happening, but I knew something really big was happening. What seemed like an hour of silence passed. It felt as if all the angels in Heaven stopped and watched. There were a million eyes on Ian at that moment, but only four human eyes.

> It felt as if all the angels in Heaven stopped and watched.

"Okay, I'll go," he said simply.

I burst into tears. My husband was going to Africa—albeit he was going to Swaziland. I didn't even know where in Africa Swaziland was, but he was going to my "homeland" in only thirty-six hours. I just knew what God had planned. He would take Ian there, rip out his heart, and plant it in Africa. I just knew it! It had to be that way so that we could then follow my passion to work in Kenya! Yea, God!

Twelve days later, Ian came home. Seemingly untouched. How could that be? He told me about the first day he went out in the field and walked up to a mud hut. Being the operations guy that he is, he was admiring the Disney-like quality of the hut. I mean, these people have gone to a lot of trouble to make this look like real mud. He described reaching forward and scratching a bit of the wall with his nail to see what it was really made of. And a chunk of mud fell off. It was real mud! These people used real mud to make the mud huts look real. Wow! What great attention to detail, he thought. Before anyone would see the missing mud, he bent down, picked up the chunk, spat on it in his hand, and then massaged it back into place. Hmmm. Mud. What a great idea.

Ian spent the week with a team of 300 Americans, mostly from a church called Shadow Mountain Community Church in southern California. He had never heard of it before, but did say that their leader, a man named Dr. David Jeremiah, was a really neat man.

As with everyone who goes to Africa, it takes a long time to begin to process what you have seen, or didn't see. And at the end of a trip I always tell people that they will have to accept that Africa is not "process-able." How can we as humans or worse yet, how can we as Christians sit for one moment and think that it is okay for a single child to die of hunger today? How? How is it okay for a single child to die of malnutrition or of scurvy (vitamin C deficiency) like in the old seafaring days because they only have cornmeal to eat? How? I ask you to stop reading at the end of this paragraph and close your eyes, put back your head and give me an answer to these questions: "Is it okay with YOU that *30,000 children will die TODAY* of hunger and malnutrition in Africa alone because they have no food or no one to go get them food?" How will you go to sleep TONIGHT knowing this? I beg you to be still and close your eyes, but open your mind to my question.

As Ian came home and tried to process what he had seen, he started with the mud hut story, but as the week went on he began to verbalize his confusion at what he had seen. He admitted that it wasn't until late in the week when he was wondering where the people who were sitting outside that mud hut went at night. Where did they live? It was his operational thinking, and his love for the brilliance of Disney World, and their attention to detail, that would not allow him to accept that people *lived* in that hut, twenty-four hours a day, seven days a week. I sat looking at him with great fascination as if looking at an interesting bug. He was wondering where they actually lived? How do you process the fact that a family of nine people live in a home made of mud? Then how do you process the fact that hundreds of millions of people living in homes constructed of mud. You can't. It's not right.

I was recently in Malawi and was leading a team of North Americans through a place called the Ngona Slum just outside of the capital of Lilongwe. As we walked through the poorest of the poor, who are actually squatters living in tiny mud homes; we were followed by throngs of children. We were like pied-pipers leading hundreds of children through the narrow pathways that were lined with tall walls of vertically-shaped mud. The children who followed us were mostly orphans and were all little children, under the age of six. The narrow path was a bit like a rat's maze, and I was careful to stay with the group because I knew there was no way I could find my way out if I fell behind.

At one point one of our volunteers casually said, "You know, this place really isn't so bad. I expected worse." These hundred or so children, who were scurrying around our feet, were living alone in homes made of mud. People had taken mud from the ground and put it in a vertical format to create a wall and then some put straw over the top to keep out the sun and rain. There are 45,000 people living in that slum and 75 percent of them are children. They are living inside vertical walls of mud (in case I haven't made that point clear), and my volunteer friend thinks "it really isn't so bad."

> There are 45,000 people living in that slum and 75 percent of them are children.

I was stunned. It's that processing thing. How do we begin to process 35,000 children living alone in mud and make it okay with us? We can't, so we don't. Instead we go back home and think to ourselves, "I don't think I am being called to Africa, and besides, I went. I made an extra donation and I hauled bags of used clothes over to give to the poor. I have done my missions thing and now I have to get back to the real world, my family, and focus on my job or I will lose it. God wouldn't want me to lose my job, would He?"

Back to Ian. Processing. Although the truth of the situation finally did come to the surface of Ian's mind, (he knew that the people lived in carved out mud, until it rained too hard and the hut was washed away), he truly didn't feel that he was called to Africa or that his heart had been left there. I was stunned. What was God doing? How could Ian not have seen the truth and said that it was *not* okay with him? The only ray of hope I had was his final story about his bus trip back to the Johannesburg airport. He was listening to his MP3 player and a song, "Here with Me" by Mercy Me started playing that brought him to tears, right there in the bus. The lyrics sang:

I long for your embrace
Every single day
To meet you in this place
And see you face to face

Will you show me?
Reveal yourself to me
Because of your mercy
I fall down on my knees

And I can feel your presence here with me
Suddenly I'm lost within your beauty
Caught up in the wonder of your touch
Here in this moment I surrender to your love

You're everywhere I go
I am not alone
You call me as your own
To know you and be known

You are holy
And I fall down on my knees

Somehow this song had broken through and touched his heart, and he wept. There was still hope. Now his focus was on finding a job and moving forward with his life. Four days later, my dad passed away.

A few months later in April, 2005, I was leading another small team back to the Mully Children's Family Home in Kenya. I was happy to continue doing the work in Kenya, while Ian was committed to finding out where he was to go next. Days before I got on a plane with my friends, we got a call from Bruce. He was wondering how Ian's trip was and if Ian had fallen in love with Africa as we had all hoped. I told him that Ian had not, but that I would never lose hope, and that I was off to Kenya.

> He still wanted us to come, but he wanted us to stay for nine weeks, and he wanted us to bring our children.

Bruce explained that he was beginning to work on the plans for a new initiative called the African Dream Village in Swaziland that would help house 10,000 orphans. Wow, how exciting! And he wondered if we could go to Swaziland to help develop it: Ian working on how to operationalize it, and me on how to market it in North America. Without much discussion, Ian said yes again and we began to make plans as I left for Kenya. After my return, Bruce called again and said that there had been some delays on the African Dream Village, but that there were more areas that his team could use some help with. He still wanted us to come, but he wanted us to stay for nine weeks, and he wanted us to bring our children, who were eight and ten years old at the time. I was stunned again. That seems to happen around Bruce. Ian said we would have to talk and pray about it, but asked, "When do you want us?"

Bruce said, "Right away—when can you come?"

We promised to call him back shortly with our answer. Three weeks later, on May 25, 2005, the Maxwell children were pulled out of their last few weeks of school and the Maxwell family was on the adventure of a lifetime as volunteers for *Dream for Africa* for nine weeks. What were we going to do? We had no idea, but we were committed to rolling up our sleeves and doing whatever needed to be done. Wash dishes? Sure. Plant vegetables? Absolutely. Play with the children? Of course. Africa here we come!

In a span of nine weeks, we moved eleven times, between two African countries, with two kids and everything we had taken for the journey. We traveled with our "adopted daughter" Helen, from MCF in Kenya, who flew on her first airplane to help watch our kids while we were in Africa. We stayed wherever we were sent and ate more Kudu (large antelope with big twisted horns) than we did beef. We didn't see a McDonalds for nine weeks because there were none. We enjoyed pap regularly and ate ostrich neck when we had to. We swerved past hundreds of goats and cattle as we drove through the hairpin turns in Swaziland and gasped at the beauty of creation at *God's Window* in South Africa.

Ian was critically instrumental in putting on a pastor's conference to an audience of 600 Swazi pastors whose first language was Siswati. I wrote a week-long series of newspaper articles for the Swazi Observer (national newspaper) on "AIDS and the Church." We celebrated Spencer's eleventh birthday in Swaziland and Chloe's ninth birthday in South Africa. We took fresh fruit and bread to a local dump to give to the children who pick through the garbage to get their daily food. We played with orphans at a children's center who go there to get their one meal a day and be safe from predators of all shapes and sizes. We even hosted teams of volunteers who had traveled from all over America to come and plant gardens. In total we met close to 2,000 new people in nine weeks and led several hundreds of them on *Never Ending Gardens* trips in countries we had never been in before. It was nuts. But we were determined to embrace the adventure and give it our all.

One day I got a friendly e-mail from a Swazi woman named Viv who had read one of my newspaper articles titled "Practice What They Preach." She was writing to encourage me and to invite me to join her woman's home care group that goes out each Friday and takes food and clothing to children who are orphaned and to people who are living or dying with AIDS. What a wonderful opportunity! I jumped at the chance and soon had made plans to meet with the ladies. They actually turned out to be angels in disguise.

We started the day at a neighborhood feeding center where local women volunteer to cook each day to provide a meal for many dozens of children who would otherwise get no food. The center was located about five kilometers from where we were staying. I had brought fresh fruit and rice to contribute to the food packs. They would be delivered to others who lived too far away or who could not walk. We then got in the vehicle that I was driving (right-hand steering wheel, left-hand stick shift, and left side of the road) and off we went. Our first visit was to see a young man, around twenty years old, who was dying of AIDS. We found him in his small house on his bed, ready for the visit. He had a pile of medicine bottles beside the bed that contained his life saving anti-retro viral medication (ARV) that he had been able to access through these home care women. His younger sister sat outside with her six-month-old baby strapped to her back. Both mother and baby also had full-blown AIDS, but neither of them were on the medication. I asked why? The answer was simple and she gave it with the same energy she would ask for sugar in her coffee. She said in Siswati, that ARVs are what actually kill you.

"What?" I exclaimed, trying to remain calm and non-judgmental. She went on to explain that everyone she knew who went on that medication died shortly afterward, so it must be the pills that are killing them. I later found out from a local doctor that ARVs are only given to people who are near death from AIDS. If they are HIV positive or are not really sick yet, they don't qualify for the drug. In fact, if people do not take the medicine at the exact time each day, or lose access to the medication, their health will deteriorate much more quickly resulting in an even faster death.

After leaving this little family, we drove another few kilometers and entered a homestead with five or six huts that could house fifty to sixty people. If I were to enter a place like this in Kenya with a motorized vehicle, there would be dozens of children and women running out to greet us. Today, there was no one. I mean *no one*. No one came to see what the noise was, who was there, or what we were doing. There were no children anywhere. Where were they? We got out of the car and walked through the huts to the last hut at the back. We were greeted by a young man in his twenties, who recognized the women I was with. These women normally traveled there on foot. He nodded and quietly took us through a dark room to see the patient, his younger brother. He lay fully clothed on his bed with one sheet to cover him. He was an older teenager who was clearly in the last stages of AIDS. For more than a month the caregiver had been trying

> He had been too weak to leave that bed for a month, and now he lay there dying and there was nothing anyone could do. But maybe there was.

to get an ambulance or medical vehicle to come and transport him to the clinic or hospital, but with no luck. He had been too weak to leave that bed for a month, and now he lay there dying and there was nothing anyone could do. But maybe there was. I asked if we could take him in my Condor (a bare bones Jeep-like vehicle commonly used in African countries).

The women seemed shocked that I would ask. But I could see by the look on their faces that it would be a good idea. We helped him get up. He was very tall, over six feet, but very weak. He couldn't stand alone. We could feel that he was just a skeleton under his vinyl tracksuit, however his ankles were the size of tree stumps from typical AIDS related swelling. We had to carry him as best we could to the car, and then gently put him on the seat without further irritating his bedsores. We took him straight to a clinic.

When we arrived we put him in a wheelchair, and his brother pushed him to the line to wait. I later found out that he would likely have to sleep on the ground outside for at least one night while he waited to see a medical person (probably not a real doctor). I do not know what happened to him after that, but I am not optimistic about his survival.

That was a tough ride, but we had one more stop to make. This one changed my life forever and threw a tanker-sized bucket of gasoline on the fire that was already burning inside me.

We drove back towards Ezulweni where we were staying at the time. When we were exactly one kilometer from our accommodations, we turned off the main road and stopped. I parked in front of a rusted chain-link fence that was ten-feet high and locked with a chain. There was just room enough for all of us to squeeze through. I wasn't quite sure why we were squeezing through when what we were really doing was trespassing into a junk yard –a real junk yard where old cars and their old parts go to die.

As I scanned the area, I spotted something moving near the building that must have been an office of some sort. I walked towards the movement with my eyes glued on what I had seen for fear of it disappearing. It reminded me of when you hit your golf ball into the tall grass and you have to remain completely focused, staring at the place it went into the grass so you don't lose it.

With that same stare, I walked down to discover that the movement was five tiny children sitting half-naked on the dirt. They were sitting in front of a long 2" by 4" board that they were pushing into the fire they had made to keep warm. A jet-black pot of rice sat precariously on top of the fire. There were nine children who lived here, and all were under the age of ten. One of the two-year-old twins sat on the lap of the six year old, who rocked the little one to keep him from crying. The other twin was being consoled by a five-year-old brother as he sat on the boy's lap, naked, except for the witch doctor's twine that was tied around his waist and a scrap of material over the top half of his torso. The three year old was totally despondent.

I asked if they had parents and learned that the mother was a prostitute and there were many fathers. The mother came to see the children every couple of weeks. Other than that, they were on their own. I had to see more, so asked if I could go inside. The ladies said that they had never gone inside because it was against their policy to enter uninvited. I said determinedly that I would go in and put the groceries inside. I carried my camera with me. Inside, I almost threw up. There was one bowl on the floor from which the children and the many stray dogs ate. There was a bedroom with a couple of straw mats and a couple of very dirty, thin blankets. That is where the children slept, along with the dogs. Next I spotted a curtain. Curious to see what was behind it, I pulled it aside and saw a beautifully-made bed covered in new satin sheets and pillow coverings: perfect for their mom's profession, and clearly out of bounds for the dogs and her children. The children had not been bathed, maybe ever. They were hungry and scared and emotionally dead, but yet they lived. I looked into the five year old's eyes as he held his little brother, and he looked straight into my heart and with his eyes asked me a simple question, "White lady, do you really care that I am here like this? Is what you see okay with you?" He had no emotion in his face, his eyes or his stare. It was simply a question. Do I care? Is it okay?

> . . . his eyes asked me a simple question, "White lady, do you really care that I am here like this? . . ."

We left the children that afternoon, and I drove the one kilometer to my warm, safe place to be with my family. I downloaded my photos and sat staring at them. To think that within walking distance of where I was going to lay my head that night, those children would be sitting in the dark, waiting . . . for what? I decided that day that it was not okay with me that this was happening. And to think that these children don't even count in the 44 percent of the total child population of Swaziland who are considered orphans. They are not included in the fifteen million AIDS orphans because they have a mother, who is likely to be HIV positive and spreading the disease to men and her children alike. I had to do something, do more, but what? Only God knew.

Chapter Eleven

SPIRIT OF ADOPTION

Our first official *Never Ending Gardens* trip turned out to be one of the craziest weeks of my life. When God shows up, the world turns upside down. We drove to White River, South Africa, from Swaziland with some trepidation. Both Ian and I had shadowed Lad Chapman (the Dream for Africa US Missionary in Swaziland) on a Never Ending Garden trip the week before. We were certain that we were unprepared and untrained to help lead the 104 Americans who were arriving from California and Colorado.

Ian was to work on the operations side of running the trip, while I was to be Julie McCoy (remember, the social director from the Love Boat?) and be the "hostess with the mostess" *and* be the master of ceremonies at the dinners every night that week. I sat uncomfortably through the orientation and tried to gather my thoughts. What are we doing here? MC what? What was the topic? Was there a format to follow? Some content to share? If there was, it had not been shared with me.

So I sat sweating. And then I was told that I was to lead morning prayer each day at 6:30 A.M. Me? Lead morning prayer? I have never led prayer in my life and I don't "do" 6:30 A.M. very well. But I had to do it, so I got up and psyched myself up and went down to the room on Monday morning. I pulled six or eight chairs into a circle, wondering who would get up that early in Africa to go and pray. One of the pastors from North Coast Calvary Chapel in San Diego,

Jeff Reinke, came in and nicely asked me what I was doing and if he could help. I said that I was pulling chairs into a circle for prayer time. He looked at me quizzically and gently reminded me that there were 104 people on the trip. I smiled and replied, "Yes, but it's not likely they are all going to get up early to pray." I admit I was a bit flippant and a bit hopeful that no one would come, since I didn't have a clue what I was doing.

Although there was no coffee in sight, Pastor Jeff and his team of ninety-plus people showed up every morning at 6:30 A.M. for prayer and proved to be quite competent and committed to prayer, devotions, and song. In fact, by Wednesday I actually looked forward to each morning with the team. However, I was convinced that God was in heaven shaking His head with His hands over His eyes thinking, "What have I done?"

After the very first morning prayer time a woman named Betsy came up to me and said that the Lord had told her she was to pray with me that week because God was preparing me for a big ministry. Although I thought she likely had the wrong person, I had learned to welcome any and all people who offered to pray for me. I figured it couldn't hurt. She had been asking the Lord why He had brought her to Africa and felt like she was there to pray for the leadership of Dream for Africa. Of course, I knew that the "leadership" that God told her about was Bruce and his leadership team, but I didn't want to discourage her by telling her that we were only lowly volunteers and, in fact, we had never been to White River before. I just accepted her prayer gratefully.

At dinner on Sunday and Monday I began my new gig as Master of Ceremonies. I would stand up and ask people how their day had been and have them share their experiences, observations, and "ah-ha" moments from being in the field. I had asked both pastors who were present to provide the scriptural "meat" of the evening as I wouldn't really know where to begin and didn't want to step into any deep spiritual water and get Bruce and the team in trouble.

I realized by Monday night that it would be a long week of just hearing testimonials. I had the sense that the volunteers who had traveled all the way from America, really didn't know the truth about what was happening in Africa. Sure they saw the poverty (which was not nearly as extreme in White River as in so many other areas in Africa). But poverty is poverty and as 314 million Africans live on less than $1.00 per day, the teams did see poverty where they were planting. Even so, I felt I was to tell them more, show them more, and pull back the curtain of truth to let them peer into the eyes and lives of the people suffering and dying from hunger, poverty, and AIDS.

> I felt I was to tell them more, show them more, and pull back the curtain of truth to let them peer into the eyes and lives of the people suffering and dying from hunger, poverty, and AIDS.

While the teams were out in the field planting on Tuesday, I prepared a PowerPoint presentation (because that is what marketing chicks do best) to give after dinner, along with a few photos from my other trips that I had put to the song "I Can Only Imagine" by Mercy Me. When I gave the presentation on Tuesday night, something very new and strange and wonderful happened. When I had finished my thirty-minute presentation, no one moved. Literally, no one moved. It was like everyone was stuck. Not a sound was made, not a body moved.

I left the room and met Ian in the lobby. He was in tears. That never happens. He's a guy. He doesn't cry, and besides, he has seen my photos a million times before without that response. I asked him what on earth he was crying about and he said, "That was unbelievable!" I was totally baffled. I mean, I thought it went well and all, but I have shown those pictures and told those stories dozens of times, but not with that response.

After a few minutes I thought maybe I should go back in the room and put on some music just to break the air a bit. When I went back in, it was like stepping into a warm bath. I could feel the Holy Spirit in the room. It was amazing! I have never felt anything quite like it. I didn't even know what the Holy Spirit felt like or if you could actually feel Him, but when I walked into that room, I knew that I knew the Holy Spirit was present. I happened to have a Michael W. Smith CD in my laptop, so I put it on to try to cut through the air a bit. No one moved for fifteen minutes. They just sat there . . . staring at nothing. Many were sobbing. Some were on the ground praying. An hour later there were people still sitting. It was crazy. People's lives were changed that night. I had been used by God. Wow!

The rest of the week was foreign to me, and not just because I was in a foreign land. Each and every day God showed up in amazing ways with words of encouragement for us. Funny thing was we didn't really know why. After all, we were just volunteers, for nine weeks, and then we would go home.

Saturday night was the last official night before part of the team flew back to the US the next day. As I walked into the restaurant, one of the very senior and influential local pastors, Lexon, stopped me by putting his hand on my arm. I had not met him before, but had seen him around all week. He said, "You have a very big ministry in Africa. You will be the voice of Bruce Wilkinson in Africa." I asked him why he would say that as Dr. Wilkinson didn't really need anyone to be his voice. Inside I actually laughed at that thought. *Me, the voice of the great teacher?* Lexon's response was that he could see the anointing all around me, and went on to say that I was to reach out to women.

The next morning a large group of us left to attend Sunday services at a local African church. Ian had to stay back to get all those people who were flying home on the bus to Johannesburg. It was our first Sunday in White River, and we were taken to the church of one of the local pastors who had been working with us all week. I was along for the ride. I did not know who the pastor was, nor did I know anyone from the church prior to that day. In fact, I was still walking around a bit dazed, not quite knowing what I was doing, supposed to be doing, or where I was to be doing it.

As I sat in this large gymnasium-type church, a white South African woman stood up at the front and started to speak. I had just sat down and was getting settled when I thought I heard her call my name from the front. I looked up to see if I knew her. I had never seen her in my life, so I looked back down and continued to pull my Bible out of my bag. My Kenyan daughter Helen, nudged me in the ribs with her arm and said, "She asked you to stand." I almost died. Again she asked, "Would Ian and Janine Maxwell please stand up." Ian wasn't even there! Who was she, and why am I standing in the middle of this church where I don't know a single soul? And how does she know my name? As I sheepishly stood at the back of the church, she began to speak to me from the very front in a loud and confident voice. She said that she had heard me speak about AIDS at one of our group dinners earlier in the week, and the Lord had given her a "word" for me. What did that mean, I thought? A word? Huh? As I stood up, this is what she said (transcribed from a video that someone took):

> I was there at your presentation on Tuesday night. The Lord spoke to me concerning the call of God and the commissioning of God. There are many of the team that received the call of God about coming to Africa that night and there are many who are to receive the commission of God to minister here.
>
> The Lord spoke to me about you and your husband. We just received a couple from America last week named Ian and Janine. And there is something about when God speaks twice.
>
> When the Lord called the prophet Samuel He said, "Samuel, Samuel." When He called Saul and Saul became Paul He said, "Saul, Saul." It is called the double enunciation of Deity. When God is about to do something profound on the earth, He calls twice. Because what He has established in heaven, He is about to establish on earth.
>
> When He called the prophet Samuel, He was doing a new work. When He called Saul, He was doing a new work. And I heard that unto you and your husband. God is calling you to release the spirit of adoption, a new dimension to your ministry. You will begin to lay hands on children and release the spirit of adoption to them, the sons and daughters of God. You have your own natural children, but God has given you "spiritual children." He is calling you to be a father and mother in the Kingdom of God, a new breed of father and mother. So don't be afraid to pray and to release the spirit of adoption in the lives of those you touch.

When she was finished, I sat down. Then her husband, who was a visiting speaker, began to give the message. He said that God's strategy in Africa is through the children, and that the hope and future of Africa lies with the next generation and the church must help the children. Then he asked us to turn to James 1:27, "Religion that God our Father considers pure and faultless is this: to look after orphans and widows in distress and keep oneself from being polluted by the world." It was the same verse that I had used at the end of my presentation earlier that week. This verse has since become my rallying cry.

> James 1:27, "Religion that God our Father considers pure and faultless is this: to look after orphans and widows in distress . . ."

After the service, I immediately went up to this woman to find out what it was that she had just done. The woman's name was Sarah Brayan and her husband was Larry. Larry had been a volunteer driver all week for the Never Ending Gardens trip and both of them serve as missionaries with their family in South Africa. Both of them had been at dinner on Tuesday night when I spoke. I had not seen either of them that evening. I had never seen Sarah before Sunday morning in church. When I spoke with her afterward, she said that she had a dream on Tuesday night after the PowerPoint presentation when God showed up. The Lord showed her that the Holy Spirit had descended on the room, and that many people were called that night. She explained that once people are called, God would start working on them and preparing them.

On Sunday morning, as she was praying, the Lord told her that Ian and I were to be commissioned. She saw us laying hands on children in Africa and "releasing the spirit of adoption" on them (see Romans 8:12–17). She went on to say that we were here to speak the truth about what is happening in Africa and that the truth will upset many people. She told me to be prepared, because we would have a very confrontational ministry by speaking the truth. Ugh.

Now remember, I am a marketing chick. I am not a pastor or a theologian or anyone who remotely qualifies for any of this. I like disco and dancing, afternoons by the pool, late nights in the hot tub, going to movies, and eating junk food. How could God have gotten this so wrong? Yes, I know I was called to Africa. Yes, I was obedient to close my business. Yes, I am here, after all. But *no!* This can't be about us. What are we supposed to do? How are we supposed to do it?

I ask you (*yes, you*) reading this book, wherever you are, to imagine what just happened. A complete stranger stands up and says a bunch of words that you can't even hear as quickly as she is saying them and then sits down. The only thing you hear is that you and your husband, who still isn't that big on Africa, are called to be a new breed of father and mother to the people you touch and that you are to lay hands on children and "release" onto them something that you have never heard of before. What would you be thinking?

The words that kept ringing over and over in my ears were "release the spirit of adoption." I am adopted. Is the spirit of adoption a good thing to release *onto* people or is it a bad thing and people were to be released *from* it? I was just so in over my head. Here I am, alone, being told that my husband and I are to do something that I don't even know if it's good or bad. Oh, brother.

Over the next many months, I got a lifetime of learning on what a prophetic word is, how to evaluate and measure it for truth. But as I learned and studied and grew, I still was baffled by this "spirit of adoption." If for no other reason than the fact that I am adopted, I at least wanted to know if it was a good or bad spirit. I sent an e-mail out to every pastor and every spiritual person I knew and asked them if they knew what it was. Some said that it was a bad spirit and one said that it was binding. Others said that it was a good spirit and one that brought us as God's children back to His family as He adopted us. But that didn't make sense because I thought I was a child of God. I always thought the Bible said that we were born as children of God. Then I called my mom to bounce these ideas off her. It was a bit tricky as she is my "adopted mom," but she is wise, well read, a very spiritual person, and I knew that she could help.

What I learned in putting together all the pieces is that each of us is born a child of God. We are in His family, just as my children are in my family as I gave birth to them. But at some point, that point where we can choose Him and His ways or not, that point of cognitive free will, He puts us up for adoption and we are adopted into the world. He still loves us and cares for us, but until we choose Him as father there is no inheritance for us as His children.

What a scary thought. Having given birth to two beautiful babies, I cannot imagine the pain that my birth mother suffered when choosing to give me away. Nine months in her belly, hours of grueling pain, the shame and isolation felt from this unwanted pregnancy at age fifteen, and then to have to give away the prize, the fruit, the reward that most of us get at the end of the birth process. To be left with nothing but an empty space in your heart for the one that you carried, talked to, and nurtured before she was born. And then to see that small face, those blue eyes and blond hair and have to give the child to the nurse so that she could be taken away to an unknown place. Would you ever see her again? Would she be safe? Would she be alone? Would she be cared for and have food and a red bicycle and nice clothes? Would she be happy and marry a nice man and have beautiful children who would be your grandchildren? I can't imagine this pain, this selfless sacrifice made by a mother so that the child has a better chance for a life.

Is this what God does? Does He really create us and give birth to us and care for us, talk to us, and nurture us only to release us to the world? The world couldn't possibly provide a better life for us than He could. Does He sit and wonder like my mother did about how I will turn out? Will I be safe? Will I be alone? Will I be happy? Does He wonder if He will ever see me again?

After a strange set of events in the summer of 2006, I had the opportunity to meet my birth mother. We met in a small restaurant and sat across the booth from each other, neither of us knowing what to think or what would happen. After she gave me up for adoption, she went on to marry and had three boys, so she sat and looked at me like you would look at an exotic bird. She tried to keep herself from staring, but then would just reach out and hold my hand to get a better look. Did it look like hers? Did I look like her? She told me that I had my father's eyes. My mother and I had met again, after forty-one years.

I thanked her for her sacrifice and for giving me up in blind faith that someone would come along and care for me. Oh, what faith. What a choice. What a permanent decision. And that is what God does for us. He allows us to be given up to the world, with hopes that we will one day come back and find Him. This is called free will.

Now, imagine the joy that my adopted mom and dad experienced when they got that phone call. A little girl has been born. She has blond hair and blue eyes, and was born perfect. No blemishes. No imperfections. She will be your daughter, and you will give her a name and care for her, they were told. You will adopt her into your family, and you won't have to worry if she is being cared for, because you will care for her. You will not have to worry if she will be safe, because you will keep her safe. You won't have to worry if she is alone, because you will be with her. Additionally, you will have the blessing of meeting her future husband and playing with your beautiful grandchildren. That is what the adopted parents get. What a blessing. But that blessing can not come without the ultimate sacrifice of the child being given up for adoption by the birth mother.

Once we reach the point that our heavenly Father gives us up to the world, He sits and longs to be the father that gets to adopt us back. When we are humanly adopted as babies, we do not make that choice, the choice is made for us by those looking out for our best interest. When we are given free will by our heavenly Father, we choose which "family" to be adopted into. We all spend time in the family called World.

> . . . when we go out searching for a better home, a better place to live, it is our Heavenly Father who stands at the end of the path with His arms wide open, much like the father who welcomed back his prodigal son . . .

This family called World also has other names. You may have met people from the family called Lust or Pride, or the ones that lived at the end of the block named Greed or Hate. I remember going to school with people who were from the family of Jealousy and Fear. But we can choose to leave those families. There is no father heading those families. There is no inheritance for the children in those families. They are all filled with orphans. There is no parent at all there.

The children in those families are not safe or secure. They are not guaranteed shelter or comfort. But when we go out searching for a better home, a better place to live, it is our Heavenly Father who stands at the end of the path with His arms wide open, much like the father who welcomed back his prodigal son in Luke 15:11–32. His arms will protect us. His very shadow will keep us safe. He is our refuge and our fortress. He keeps us safe at night and keeps the arrows away from us during the day. He even brings angels with Him to surround us all the time. (Psalm 91) What a life that is. What a successful adoption story that is.

As I sat and pondered this revelation, my heart began to break open for the children of Africa. It is impossible for us to begin to get our heads around fifteen million children living without parents. What safety and security do they have? Where do they find comfort when they are afraid or being chased down? Who can they run to? Their fathers are most certainly dead, and in most cases their father's illness has killed their mother too. What is their inheritance? The children whom I have seen and met have been adopted into families named Shame and Guilt and I know many who are named Fear and Anger. Can these children also be adopted by our heavenly Father? Of course they can and He longs for them to choose Him, but how would they know about Him? Who would tell them? And then I remembered the words that were spoken in South Africa:

> God is calling you to release the spirit of adoption—a new dimension to your ministry. You will begin to lay hands on children and release the spirit of adoption to them, the sons and daughters of God. You have your own natu-

ral children, but God has given you spiritual children. He is calling you to be a father and mother in the Kingdom of God—a new breed of father and mother.

Is this possible? Could this be what I am being called to do? I am a marketing chick. Help me, Jesus.

Chapter Twelve

SITTING DUCKS

It was July, and we had passed the halfway mark of our volunteer time commonly referred to by Ian as "sixty-six days in Africa." Although it was an adventure, I have to say there were things that had me quite on edge. It wasn't the travel or the many moves, but it was that the left hand did not know about what the right hand was doing at Dream for Africa.

Now this is not a unique problem to any organization, but I guess I thought that things would be running smoother. Bruce and his wife, Darlene Marie, had decided to move from Johannesburg, South Africa, to Ezulweni, Swaziland, as a show of commitment to the people of Swaziland and the ministry there. On June 30 they had their things packed and on July 1 they were in Swaziland where Spencer, Chloe, and Helen had a great day helping Darlene Marie unpack and set up house. Later that night they drove back to South Africa and then flew home, as they had originally planned. I am not sure how they did it, having a home in two places on opposite sides of the world, but they did, and always had a smile, a word of encouragement, and a big hug for all they came in contact with.

Although everyone was crazy-busy, I did feel that we had full access to the Wilkinson's to discuss the stresses of working in Africa, the differences in culture, and other problems that arose. There was no shortage of awareness on how impossible the tasks at hand were, but there was equally no shortage of faith that God was on the throne and would direct their every path. I can honestly say that I was sitting in the cheap seats, listening to the typical chatter about life inside the organization, hearing people's frustrations with this and that, but knowing safely that it didn't really affect me. I was just a volunteer, and in a few short weeks I would have my feet back on Canadian soil and begin my work with MCF again.

Being in Africa for the summer was a truly spectacular experience. We learned so much about working on the ministry side instead of the business side. (Yes, I had to learn to be a bit nicer, calmer, and patient. Ugh!) We learned so much more about these different African countries—real statistics from real hospitals and government representatives. And we learned how to be flexible as individuals and to work together as a family under less than ideal circumstances. I also learned many things that I thought would be transferable to my work in Kenya. The bottom line of this is that we went full out, gave 110 percent in all we did as servants to those who needed us and we clung to each other as to a life raft to get through the turbulent times.

We were back in White River for the second trip that included volunteers from San Diego and Wichita Falls (among many other places, including Canada). We got a phone call from the Chief Operating Officer at Dream for Africa saying he was driving up from Johannesburg to talk to us. It was a five-hour drive. Oh boy, what did we do? I was sure that I had said something desperately inappropriate to someone. I have a chronic condition of "foot in mouth" disease. I've had it since I was young. But he assured us that there was nothing bad, he just wanted to talk. I still felt sick from my other chronic condition called paranoia. He arrived and as we sat and talked, the question finally came.

"We would like to offer you both jobs at Dream for Africa. Ian, you would be Director of Operations Globally for the Never-Ending Gardens initiative. Janine, you would be Director of Recruitment and be focused on filling the future trips with people from America." Then he just grinned at us, waiting for our response.

> "We would like to offer you both jobs at Dream for Africa. . . ."

I have to admit my initial thinking was *Has this guy had a stroke? This organization is a bit dysfunctional right now (it was in the start-up stages and had been hugely successful to that point, but it had a long way to go) and you want us to come now? You have got to be kidding. We need to step into a safe, easy job. We have already done the hard stuff.* As time passed, we learned that almost everyone in the organization thought we were there as volunteers specifically to test the waters and then join the team. It never occurred to them that we weren't going to be full-time employees. And frankly, it never occurred to us that we would.

It seems logical, looking at it from hindsight, but we sure hadn't thought about it with foresight. Frankly, it made a ton of sense for Ian to fill that role. He would be great at it. He is operationally excellent and is a great problem-solver. He likes to play complicated games and solve puzzles that otherwise seem unsolvable. Ian was a big part of ONYX's success because he was able to make the crazy ideas that the team came up with, work. He even helped come up with some of the crazy ideas, that weren't so crazy after all. But they were successful. In this way ONYX had a strong point of differentiation from our clients because we really did think out of the box and we gave our clients a leg up on their competitors. However, it didn't seem to make sense at all for me to be Director of Recruitment. I would be booking Bruce into speaking engagements in America (where I don't live or really know anyone) and then slowly I would begin to do the speaking myself as Bruce went on to do other parts of the initiatives. That just didn't sound possible. But in the end I agreed to try it for six months—that meant until January 2006. At that point, things would need to be revisited. And so they were. We accepted the positions offered with great trepidation and with an equal sense of excitement that the journey had just begun.

I remember telling the kids about the job offers and they went crazy with excitement. And then the questions began; all the questions that pertained to their lives. These were all the questions for which we had no answers. I was driving in Swaziland with Spencer one day when he started peppering me with questions. Where will we live? Will we live in Swaziland? Will we live in South Africa? Will we live in Atlanta? Where will we go to school? When do they start school in Atlanta? Don't they start school in January in Africa? If they start school in January, will I skip to the next grade? Can I get my own computer?

It went on and on and with each new question, they got the same old answer. I don't know. I couldn't answer any of them. I didn't have a clue. So I finally turned to Spencer and laughed and said, "Spencer, I can't answer any of your questions because I just don't know." Spencer is the planner in the family so he likes to have everything in order and have a plan so that he knows the when, where, and how of each situation that he will face. There was a pause and then a small "hmmm" that came from the other side of the car. I looked at him and saw a complete calm come over his face, and I thought I saw a twinkle in his eye. I asked, "What does

"Isn't it cool that God knows . . . so we don't have to?"

'hmmm' mean?" And he said to me, "Isn't it cool?" Of course I asked what he meant by that and he explained, "Isn't it cool that God knows . . . so we don't have to?" Tears flowed out of my eyes (as they are now while I type this), and I realized that this was the faith of a child. This is how God wants us all to feel about Him and His plan. His plan for us is perfect, but we often think that our plan and our planning is better. As Christians we must stop and decide if we truly believe that God's plan for us is better than our plan could ever be. After all, He made us. If we believe that God's plan is the best for us, then we must have faith in our Father like the faith of a child. Like the faith of Spencer that "God knew," and Mommy didn't and that was okay. No, better yet, that was "cool."

The Maxwell Family African Summer Adventure 2005 was over—all sixty-six days. We packed up in August and said our good-byes to everyone we had met. We flew home to Canada, sent our children to Ian's parents in Ottawa, and immediately turned around and flew back to Africa. I went to Kenya to lead my last Hopes & Dreams Team group to MCF, while Ian went to Swaziland to host 349 people from Dr. Robert Schuller's Crystal Cathedral church in Southern California. These people had signed up for a trip when they heard Bruce speak at their church.

I was only leading a small team of thirty, but it included some VIPs, specifically my mom who bravely traveled in a wheelchair, and my seventy-nine-year-old Aunt Susie who had always wanted to do a missions trip. Days into our work in Kenya, I had to leave them on the farm with the Mullys and fly down to Swaziland to speak at a few of the Dream for Africa dinners. I then flew back up to Kenya, picked up my family and friends, and flew home to get our children.

The following week the kids went back to school (Hallelujah!), and Ian and I began to prepare for a wonderfully relaxing holiday. We had been invited by many of the people from North Coast Calvary Chapel, whom we had met in White River, to come to San Diego for a holiday. *Wow!* What a holiday it was!

It was Ian's fortieth birthday—a biggie. These people, whom we had just met, treated us like a king and a queen. Our new friend, Kristi, threw a party for Ian at the San Diego Yacht Club—three slips from the clubhouse—on her husband's racing boat. We were able to invite ten other new friends for a sunset cruise, and then dinner was catered on the dock. Unbelievable! We were doted on by our gracious hosts, Annely and Greg, and each and every day was more special than the day before (although the whole yacht club thing was hard to top). Our first night in San Diego, we were invited out for dinner, right down at the water against the breakers with Jeff and Robin Reinke and Buz and Marion Buzbee, whom we just adored from the trip. Along with having a great evening of laughter and stories about our African adventures, they wanted us to meet their senior pastor and his wife, Mark and Jan Foreman. We all got along famously and laughed until we almost cried from the first minute we sat down. The evening was magical as we watched the sun slowly drop into the ocean.

After a couple hours of talk, a serious moment came when Mark started to ask us questions about the ministry. Some of them were easy, and some were tough. After all, we weren't ministry people; we were marketing people who happened to be hired into a ministry. Plus we were very new and weren't sure we could answer his questions. But he continued. Pastors, as well as more than 150 members from their church, went on a Never Ending Gardens trip to South Africa and were transformed. If North Coast Calvary Chapel was going to partner with Dream for Africa, he wanted to know us, what was in our hearts and where we saw the organization and partnership progressing. With each question I felt tenser until the last one was asked.

Mark looked at us both and asked, "What would happen if the leadership at Dream for Africa changed?"

Ian and I looked at him quizzically and then looked at each other with the same confused look. What did he mean "leadership changed." The leadership would never change. That was impossible. God had called Dr. Wilkinson to Africa. He ripped out his heart and planted it there. He will always be the leader. But we didn't say those things out loud. We paused, looked at each other, and said almost in unison, "We are followers of Jesus Christ, not Bruce Wilkinson. We believe God has called us to work there and we will stay as long as He directs us to, no matter who runs it. But that doesn't matter, because Bruce will never leave." All week Ian and I chatted about what a wonderful dinner that was, but what a strange question Mark had asked. It almost seemed inappropriate, but wasn't. Mark did not know Bruce,

> Mark looked at us both and asked, "What would happen if the leadership at Dream for Africa changed?"

nor did he have any hidden reason to ask the question other than he wanted to be confident in the people he was looking at eyeball to eyeball. As the week progressed, we talked through that possibility and were sure that we would want to stay at Dream for Africa no matter what, because we were called there, and our hearts were there. Not that anything would ever happen.

One week later we flew the red-eye home from San Diego. After we arrived home, I was taking a mid-afternoon red-eye nap when the phone rang. It was Bruce. He and Ian spoke for a long time. Then Ian sat on the edge of the bed and gave me the news. Bruce was stepping down from Dream for Africa. He had spent much time in prayer and received much confirmation that he was being called back home to the US, and he was asking Ian to become President of Dream for Africa. Bruce would remain on the Board and would still do some speaking engagements for us and support the ministry, but he was leaving.

The leadership at Dream for Africa was changing, and my husband was going to be the new leader. I fell on the floor beside the bed and lay in a fetal position and sobbed with extreme apprehension. It had been a long time since I had felt excited about the prospect of working again. After ONYX closed, I didn't think I would ever be able to work again. I was broken, used up, finished. I had nothing left to offer anyone. But when the job offers were made to join Dream for Africa, I began to think about the opportunity to serve alongside and learn from Dr. Wilkinson, and it brought hope to my broken heart. I could work to bring people to the continent of Africa, where my heart resides, while truly learning about the Bible and Christ's teaching from a man who had spent his life learning about them.

This job was supposed to have been perfect. Bruce would lead the way, Ian would operationalize it, and I would promote it, and travel home to Africa. How much better could a calling be? But now? Bruce is gone. Ian is going to be the president of a US ministry whose work is based in Africa? I am the Director of Recruitment, to do what? Book Ian's speaking engagements in large US churches? Yeah, right. Ian hates public speaking. So how is that going to work? He still wasn't that big on Africa, to tell you the truth. The rug had been pulled out from under me, and frankly, my roof had just collapsed.

For the sixteen years that I was president of ONYX, the buck always stopped with me. It was my head at which people took shots (they usually missed and hit my heart instead). I took the frontline hits for sixteen years of business. In the end, I didn't have the energy to fight the fight. I couldn't handle any more criticism or pettiness of any kind. I had been looking forward to working with a man with a big reputation and thick skin who could take all those bullets for me while I got busy and did the work under his protection. My protector was leaving. And I hadn't even really started working with him yet. How could he leave? God told him to? Well, what about me? And Ian is going to be president?

I felt betrayed and quickly slid back into my hopelessness. I knew that Ian had huge potential and could do amazing things if he stepped up. But how would he be able to lead a ministry? He's an operations guy. He didn't study missions or ministry or the Bible for that matter. If Ian said yes to becoming president, we would be sitting ducks, just ready to be shot at from the bushes. And what would my role be? My role would stay the same. Ian would be the person in leadership leading the charge, and I would also continue to fulfill my role as dutiful wife and mother (yes, you can read a touch of angst in those words).

We called our new spiritual advisors and friends in San Diego and were reminded of the question that Mark had asked us exactly one week before, "What would happen if the leadership changed at Dream for Africa?" Our answer was, and is, that we are followers of Jesus Christ, not followers of Bruce Wilkinson, and that we had been called to work at Dream for Africa. Ian said yes to the job offer and was immediately made president. After all, Bruce wasn't going away, he was just stepping down as president. It would be okay.

> Ian said yes to the job offer and was immediately made president.

Several weeks later Bruce called Ian back again and told him that the Lord had given him further instructions. Bruce was to completely step down from Dream for Africa and its board. Although he loves us and will always support us and our children, he would no longer be able to speak for Dream for Africa or be associated with it. He was retiring. He was going to buy a couple of dirt bikes, grow a beard, and enjoy his wife, kids, and grandchildren. His decision was made, and it was final. And frankly, he deserved it.

Ian was now on his own. He had to build a new Board of Directors in each country and start a Canadian charity so that we could work in Canada and take people on trips from Canada. He had to deal with the legalities of changing ownership in the US, South Africa, and Swaziland, and he had to learn about the laws in each of those countries, transferring monies (or not). He had to become a human resources person and get to know the internal team and manage the departure of some people who were no longer required. But the hardest part was dealing with the rumors that surrounded Bruce's retirement.

I will add a footnote here right in the middle of the story. I am sorry to report that never in all my years of marketing, dealing with the rumors and speculation of drugs and sex and rock and roll in the advertising industry, did I ever see such a flurry of vultures circling like I did when Bruce made his retirement announcement. Never have I seen attacks like the ones that the Christian community launched against Bruce and Dream for Africa.

There was speculation and gossip spoken about him in Christian circles and lies written about him in Christian publications. When they couldn't reach him, they called us, but often didn't ask questions relevant to the work or the future of Dream for Africa. They just wanted to know the gossip. I was shocked and saddened by this. I am not suggesting that Bruce is perfect, nor would he profess that. But I do believe that the Christian community watched with baited breath to see if another great man of God had fallen. Shame on us! If that is the kind of salt that we are bringing to flavor the world, it is no wonder the world tastes so bad.

By January, 2005, Ian was president of Dream for Africa in the US, Canada, South Africa, and Swaziland and his head was spinning. What was he doing? He wasn't equipped or trained to do this. Fear and doubt began to fill our home. It was awful. And then we had churches calling to cancel trips to Africa, because they had felt betrayed by Bruce, even though it was God who called them. Our heads were spinning. How could this be? Did God make a mistake? He must have . . . but He doesn't make mistakes.

On January 28, 2006, Bruce was in Unionville, Ontario, (just north of Toronto and only 15 minutes from our home) fulfilling a speaking engagement at Unionville Alliance Church that had been scheduled many months prior. It was exactly one year to the day from when Bruce had asked Ian to go to Swaziland with him. Our friends and families attended to meet the man who had had such an impact on our family and to hear this well-known speaker.

> He then asked Ian to bend on one knee and Bruce proceeded to figuratively remove the mantle of Dream for Africa from his back, and while physically gesturing, he placed it on Ian's shoulders.

When Bruce was at the end of his message, he asked Ian to go to the front of the church. Ian obeyed and walked up. The church fell silent. No one knew who Ian was or where he was from or what he was doing there. This was not our home church. We had never been there before. But as Ian put his foot on the top step of the platform, there was a spirit of anticipation that blew like a warm breeze through the room. Bruce told the congregation a fraction of our testimony, how we had closed our business and were seeking God's will in our lives. He then asked Ian to bend on one knee and Bruce proceeded to figuratively remove the mantle of Dream for Africa from his back, and while physically gesturing, he placed it on Ian's shoulders. He prayed over Ian and anointed him with oil. It was official. Ian was now running Dream for Africa, a ministry to help the poor in Africa started by Dr. Bruce Wilkinson. We were sitting ducks. This was impossible.

That night after Bruce had flown home and the kids were in bed, we went downstairs to the far corner of our basement to escape. I remember hearing the Casting Crowns song called "The Voice of Truth." The words said:

Oh what I would do to have
The kind of strength it takes to stand before a giant
With just a sling and a stone,

Surrounded by the sound of a thousand warriors
Shaking in their armor,
Wishing they'd have had the strength to stand.

But the giant's calling out my name
And he laughs at me,
Reminding me of all the times
I've tried before and failed.
The giant keeps on telling me
Time and time again. "Boy, you'll never win!"
"You'll never win!"

But the stone was just the right size
To put the giant on the ground,
And the waves they don't seem so high
From on top of them lookin' down.
I will soar with the wings of eagles
When I stop and listen to the sound of Jesus
Singing over me.

The voice of truth tells me a different story
The voice of truth says, "Do not be afraid!"
The voice of truth says, "This is for My glory"
Out of all the voices calling out to me
I will choose to listen and believe the voice of truth

I was afraid: afraid that Ian would fail; afraid that we did not stand a chance. And frankly, I was questioning my role. Where did I fit? Bruce anointed Ian as the president, not me. And after much soul-searching, I knew that I truly did not want that position. Ian has so many gifts that he would bring to the role, plus he is a man (which can help in Africa), and frankly, I had done my time. It was his turn. But surely, God wanted me to play a role here. I'm the African Queen. It is my heart that bleeds for the people of Africa. It is me who lays awake at night seeing their faces and thinking about how I can help them next. Did God forget about me?

On February 1, 2006, we changed the name of Dream for Africa to Heart for Africa. We felt that there was a significant distinction between our dream for others and us having a heart for others. The heart is the organ that pumps the blood through the body to the hands and feet. We, as Heart for Africa, are in the unique position to pump passion for the people of Africa into the people in North America, and specifically into the Body of Christ.

The heart can live without a hand, but a hand cannot live without a heart. As Christians we are called to be the hands and feet of Christ. In Matthew 25 we are clearly given instruction to go and *feed* the hungry, *bring* drink to the thirsty, *give* shelter to the homeless, *clothe* the naked, and *visit* those who are sick and in the hospital. These are all verbs, action words, instructions on what we are to do. But it is hard to do any or all of those things without a heart for the people.

God called us to have a heart for His people in Africa and that heart began to beat for the first time on February 1, 2006.

Chapter Thirteen

A HEART FOR AFRICA

The first six months of this ministry life was filled with learning and growing and legalities and regulations. It wasn't much fun, and I couldn't help but feel that we weren't really doing anything to help the people. I do understand and have a healthy respect for the process and the laws of the land (and making the two work together), but I also have a burning knowledge that every three seconds a child dies of hunger. So each day that we worked on how Heart for Africa was to function as a non-profit organization in multiple countries, I was acutely aware that 30,000 more children had died of hunger or malnutrition. That was still not okay with me.

The old organization had focused on hunger, orphans, poverty, and AIDS, but the marketing chick in me knew that we needed an acronym that worked so we changed it to hunger, orphans, poverty, and education. In fact, it is our belief that education is the key to ending hunger, the orphan problem, poverty, and AIDS. Education had to be added, and it was. Now we were focused on hunger, orphans, poverty, education: HOPE.

Our next step was to design a logo. Well, I was qualified to do that. In fact, I had a logo sketched out in my notepad from months back, which ended up being the logo that we now use. I guess maybe I still have a little bit of marketing left in me, but I didn't trust it and got everyone's opinion and approval prior to moving forward. So now we were Heart for Africa, a faith-based humanitarian relief organization focused on bringing HOPE in the areas of hunger, orphans, poverty and education in Africa. That worked.

The next challenge was that we had a great initiative for Hunger, Never Ending Gardens, and we had a hugely successful initiative for Education called "Beat the Drum," an AIDS-specific program that educates students in school using the powerful movie called *Beat the Drum*. But there was nothing designed for orphans or poverty. Furthermore, we had to be careful not to separate the four problems because they are inextricably linked. None of the four HOPE initiatives will work well if independent of each other. The lack of access to education increases the HIV/AIDS infection rate due to ignorance of the issue.

In 2005 it was recorded that seventy-five percent of girls between the ages of fifteen and twenty-four in sub-Saharan Africa do not know that AIDS is a sexually transmitted disease. AIDS leads to poverty because the parents can't go to work because they are too sick. Poverty leads to hunger because there is no money to buy food so the women and girls are forced to prostitute themselves for money or bread. Prostitution leads to AIDS and the spreading of AIDS. AIDS leads to death which leaves orphans. Orphans can't work so they have no money which leads to hunger and more poverty. Without income the children can't pay their school fees and therefore don't get an education which leads to ignorance. Ignorance coupled with free time (no job, no school) leads to unprotected sexual activi-

> In 2005 it was recorded that 75 percent of girls between the ages of 15 and 24 in sub-Saharan Africa do not know that AIDS is a sexually transmitted disease.

ties and/or prostitution, which leads back to AIDS, death, orphans, and the cycle starts to spin faster. Our attempt to bring HOPE to an area must be as comprehensive as possible. Could we do this?

No, we couldn't. It's too much. It's too big. It's impossible. So I would go to bed, discouraged and depressed, and get up the next day to take another run at it. After all, I kept being reminded that our God is the God of the impossible, and we need God-sized solutions for these God-sized problems.

One rainy Sunday afternoon, Chloe and I decided to close the curtains and curl up on the living room couch, eat chips, and watch a movie. Chloe was ten years old at the time and hadn't seen the movie called *The Hiding Place*. *The Hiding Place* is the story of a brave Christian family named Ten Boom who lived in Holland during WWII. They were committed to saving Jews who were being rounded up and sent to Nazi concentrations camps and certain death. As the story goes, the Ten Booms hid many people upstairs in the apartment above their watch shop until one day they were betrayed. Although their hiding place was never found, the Ten Boom family was sent to prison. All but one family member named Corrie died there. Chloe had never heard this story—at least not to the depth that she was now watching it revealed on the screen. She was caught between whether it was real or whether they were actors. I tried to explain that it was a true story being re-enacted by actors.

She understood. That was not a complicated concept for a media-savvy ten-year-old. What I couldn't explain was that six million Jews were murdered, along with many other people groups just because of their religion, race, or color. She didn't understand. Neither did I. I remember as a child hearing for the first time about the Holocaust. Even though I was young, I was shocked at the injustice that was allowed to continue for so long by the rest of the world. I asked my parents how everyone could sit by for seven years and watch six million people go up in smoke and not do something. I have heard stories of the physical ashes from the concentration camps covering the houses and windows of people for hundreds of miles. There was a part of me when I was young that held my own parents accountable for not doing anything. They were alive, why didn't they help? Okay, so they were less than ten years old at the time, but why didn't my grandparents do something? Why have I not heard about the heroics of my grandfather who risked his life like the Ten Boom family to save the Jews? How could the world sit back for so long and not stand up and fight for this injustice?

I looked at Chloe and knew in the every fiber of my being that one day her generation will ask the question of my generation. They will look at us and say, "Mommy, how could you sit by for seven years and watch three million people die of AIDS each year (*twenty-one million people in seven years*) when the disease could be treated and prevented? They could have been saved. How could you live in our big house and go out for a fancy dinner every Friday while the children who were left behind were dying of hunger? Why didn't you do something?" Chloe's generation will have the right to demand an explanation. So we must find a solution.

> They will look at us and say, "Mommy, how could you sit by for seven years and watch three million people die of AIDS each year . . ."

My resolve became even more steadfast, we had to move swiftly. But what can one person do? I mean one normal person, like me? Sure, Bono can make a difference because he is a rock star, has access to buckets of cash, and also has access to the President of the United States (arguably the most powerful man in the world). I know Oprah is making a difference in South Africa by building schools for girls, but she makes a squillion dollars a year (arguably the most powerful woman in the world). Of course, people will hear her voice. But what about Stephen Lewis? He gave his heart and soul to the cause as the United Nations Special AIDS Envoy for HIV/AIDS in Africa. He stood up and screamed and yelled and wrote papers and a book, *Race Against Time* (a must read). He spoke the truth to world leaders and the World Bank, to the World Health Organization and the World Food Programme. He also sat and watched mothers die in Swaziland while listening to gogos beg for food for their grandchildren, and yet nothing happened—or did it? He was fired from the UN, or should I say that his contract was not renewed. Too much racket. Too much death. Too much truth. Too much accountability for the world leaders. May God richly bless Mr. Stephen Lewis and may his voice of truth never be silenced. So if that is true, and it is, what difference can one normal person really make?

As Ian and I struggled with this question, we were also bombarded with naysayers (mostly, if not all, from the church) who would send daily e-mails of disdain pointing out that they had heard through people in Africa that many of our gardens had died. Or they would question who was following up with the Africans to make sure they watered their gardens properly. Or better yet, how do we know for sure that the kids who sign up for abstinence really aren't having sex after all? How can we prove it to them? It was so discouraging and frustrating to receive these letters and it was so demeaning to know that they looked down on us for doing our very best, even when our best wasn't enough. We even had many people write and criticize us for not following up with them and their feelings after they had traveled to Africa with a team. We should have been there to wipe their eyes and help them deal with their pain. "*What about the pain of the children who are still in Africa?*" I screamed out loud as I read their scathing messages.

I do not want to underestimate the transformation that begins to happen when your heart gets ripped out of your body in Africa, but we do have churches and pastors and counselors and family members and even Oprah who can help us deal with our grief. The children whom we have been called to serve have no one. My focus remained on them. I was so hurt and shocked at these attacks, I must admit it really set me off my tracks and made me seriously reconsider whether I could really work in ministry. People just don't do that in business because they are focused on making money. Imagine if we all focused on solving the problems rather than pointing the finger. Lord, please forgive us.

> . . . as Christians, we must ask, "What does God want me to do?

So where should we begin? We needed a plan. Knowing that powerful people like Bono, Oprah, President Clinton, and Bill Gates had their eyes on this problem, it was easy to think that anything we could do would be insignificant. We had to ask ourselves, "What is our part in this?" And then, as Christians, we must ask, "What does God want me to do? What is my specific role? What is my little piece of the puzzle?" So Ian and I asked those questions as individuals, as a family, and on behalf of our new organization.

First Corinthians 12 talks about us being the body of Christ. We are each to have our role, and one is not greater than the other. The eye is as important as the hand. The hand cannot see, and the eye cannot hold, but they are both critical to the body. So what is the role of Heart for Africa to be? Would it be enough if we were able to provide self-sustainable food security to a family of fifteen orphans so they could provide for themselves and maybe even sell food for funds to pay for education? Absolutely! (This is "the one" solution.) But wouldn't it be great if we could multiply that model and provide self-sustainable food security for a nation? Even a little nation like Swaziland with only one million people? Would that be big enough? Of course. What about rolling that idea out to the next country and the next, all the while doing it with "the one" child in "the one" hut? Yes, it is not complicated.

And what about the orphans? We have come alongside our first children's home in Swaziland called El Shaddai. The critics shouted out, "But you're only helping thirty-two children in that home! What about the rest?" Well, what about the rest? Is helping to feed, clothe, shelter, and educate thirty-two children enough for me? Absolutely. Would it be great if we had enough volunteers and support to come along side the New Hope Children's Home with 100 more children? That would be great! And with each new group of volunteers we can support more and more homes.

But then I ask the question, "What about the children who aren't lucky enough to be in a home—in fact, most of the fifteen million orphans in Africa?" Well, what about them? What can we do? We can't build children's homes quickly enough to house all of the children who are in need. In fact, in many countries if the children leave their homes, they will lose the rights to their property (their only inheritance), so they want to stay in their village if they can.

Imagine this, if you will. You make a decision that you are going to help. You get on a plane and fly to an African country that you have never heard of before. Let's call it Malawi. Smack dab in the middle of Africa where you have never ever thought of going. You are greeted by African women singing their hearts out while hoisting your bags into the back of a truck. You head to your comfortable and safe hotel, find out you can drink all the bottled water you like, *and* you can eat the lettuce! So far, better than a Mexican vacation. At dinner you hear a bit about the local culture and customs as you enjoy a buffet that doesn't have a single wild animal or snake on the menu. And then you have a warm shower and go to sleep. When you awake, you have a lovely breakfast of your usual yogurt and granola (yep, even in Africa) and your husband (who decided at the last minute to join you) gets his fill of bacon and eggs. Now for the good part. You get in the van and head out to your first village.

> . . . imagine being welcomed by hundreds of children who greet your van with their African song and dance and are just happy that you came.

Next, imagine being welcomed by hundreds of children who greet your van with their African song and dance and are just happy that you came. No strings attached. They aren't expecting gifts or food or clothing or anything. Honestly. They just heard you were coming and came to greet you (and see you)! Imagine. Love, without anything expected in return—an almost impossible concept to understand.

And then imagine being introduced to one of the families that you have come to help. The eldest is a fifteen-year-old boy who cares for nine younger siblings, and two of his younger sisters have babies. Their father has been dead for several years, and they just buried their mother one year ago that very week. This family of children is bouncing up and down because they are so excited to see you. The littlest ones, who are big enough to walk, grab onto your fingers, and you find yourself with three children on each side. The older ones lead the way to their home while carrying the babies. They have half a roof on their hut, and the door was broken down by the same man who raped and impregnated both of the sisters. There is a cooking pot on the ground inside, but only a small bag of *Nshima* (cornmeal flour) that the home care worker brings them to eat.

Imagine spending the day with the children digging a garden, showing them with an instructor how to use the drip irrigation system that you brought them to water their gardens. Imagine putting a new roof on their hut with the help of the other Malawians who have come to assist you. Your husband repairs the door and makes their home secure. You give each of them a pair of shoes that your next door neighbor dropped off before you left home. And wouldn't you know it? Each and every pair fits one of those precious children perfectly. You leave them at the end of the day also with used clothes that you brought from home, a blanket, some fresh fruit and vegetables, and, of course, the most priceless gift of all—a soccer ball. You pray with them, hug them, encourage them, and love them. And then you go back to your hotel for a warm shower and sleep.

Is that enough? Your mind races. What about their education? What about follow up? What about AIDS testing and medical help and their clothes for next year? What about the rapist? Do they have a church? Do they have access to fresh water? What about the other fifteen million? What about, what about, what about?......STOP IT!

Was bringing that one family HOPE enough for you? If
not, you are probably asking all the questions I have listed
above and a hundred more I didn't and saying that what you
did is not enough. If it's not enough for you, then do more.
If you can't do more, then stop making yourself crazy and
imagine receiving a letter like this:

Dear Mrs. Maxwell,
I want to thank you and your friends for flying all the way
to Malawi to put a roof on my house. I can't believe that
someone would do that for me. As you know, my brothers
and sisters and I don't have a mother or father anymore,
we just have each other. But then you came and it was
like having our mom and dad with us again, even just for
a day. What you did for us changed our lives. We had no
hope and then you were there. We saw the love in your
eyes. You must love us to have come so far, just for us. Just
to fix a roof and a door and plant a garden—for a bunch
of children? Who could imagine such a thing? Not me
that's for sure. You may not believe this, another group
of people heard what your friends from America did and
they came to see our new home! We have been told that
they are now going to put a bore hole in our village, only
a few steps from our hut. Can you imagine? My sisters
walk almost six kilometers each day to get water for us,
and it is pretty dirty, but now we will have clean water
almost right in our house—just because you came to visit
us. My little brother thinks that you are angels (I think
because some of you were Azungu's and he had never
seen a white person before). I asked him why he thought
you were angels and he said, "We were hungry, and they
brought us food. We were thirsty and had to walk a long
way for water, and now we have clean water to drink.
We didn't have any warm clothes for when it gets cold
at night, and they brought us clothes and shoes that fit!

They flew here from so far away, just to visit us. They must be angels." I don't know what we did to deserve your kindness, but our lives have been changed forever. Thank you from the bottom of our hearts. We love you and pray for you every night.

Love from your son,
Mposa (which means trouble)

Now, imagine a movement of people: dozens, hundreds, thousands going and helping all the Mposa's in Malawi and all the Lillians in Kenya and all the Kantwas in Zambia, one roof at a time. One pair of shoes at a time. One bore hole at a time. One school at a time.

> It's not okay with me anymore that your children are dying in front of you from hunger, and that you are naked and that your husband died of AIDS.

Imagine people being brave enough to stop saying, "Oh, I don't think I could handle seeing the children that way. I would just cry all day. I couldn't possibly go." That won't help them. And it won't help you. I encourage you to be brave.

Imagine people being honest enough to stop saying, "I don't have the money to go to Africa," and instead they stop ordering in pizza and buying coffee every morning on the way to work. Imagine not buying *any* new clothes for a year. None. I encourage you to be honest (and stop shopping!).

Imagine people being willing to open up their hearts to the people in Africa and saying to them and to the world, "It's not okay with me anymore that your children are dying in front of you from hunger, and that you are naked and that your husband died of AIDS. It is just not okay with me! And I am going to do something about it." I encourage you to be willing and say it to one person today. Imagine the grass-roots movement that you could be one small part of that will help one child, one family, one village, one nation. You can do it. I encourage you to "just do it!"

So Ian and I sat and wrote the plan and then wondered, could one person having a heart for Africa really save a continent? The answer was simply, yes.

Chapter Fourteen

CHIEF JAMBULANI

As I reflect back on the past five years, I can see how much has happened, how my faith in God has grown, and how much my personal relationship with my heavenly Father has strengthened. I always had faith that there was a God and had accepted Him as my personal Savior when I was young. But I was not prepared for the size of Him and the size of His love for me. I never thought that I would be writing to you, a stranger, and speaking the words that I am speaking. I cannot believe God's tenacity in continuing to pursue me even when I have failed Him over and over again.

Five years ago I loved my church, but didn't read my Bible. I loved my children, but hadn't given them completely back to God for His purposes. I loved my life, or thought I did, but didn't realize that I was created for His purpose and pleasure, not for mine. My journey has all been uphill, but I can say that I have felt His presence beside me, encouraging me all the way. When I asked Him for help, He would send the most unlikely people to help me. When I took the time to ask Him for direction, He always gave it. The key for me was to take the time to ask Him because He wants us to ask. He is our Father and He wants to give. But the larger lesson was that after I asked, I had sit quietly and wait for His answer. "Be still and know that I am God" (Psalm 46:10). His answers were rarely the ones that I was looking for, but they were always "exceeding abundantly" better in the end. Always.

In March, 2006, I was in Hawaii at the HIM Conference (Hawaiian Islands Ministry) where I had the privilege of meeting Stephen Lungu. Stephen's testimony is written in his book called *Out of the Black Shadows* (another must-read book). In it he shares his life story, which is similar to that of my friend Mully.

Stephen was seven years old when his mother abandoned him, his younger brother, and his baby sister in a crowded market in Zimbabwe (then called Rhodesia). He tells a gripping story of pain and fear while living under a bridge for most of the first twenty years of his life. He and his gang called The Black Shadows reigned terror on people with their knives, guns, and hatred. His transformation is nothing less than miraculous as he finds himself at a tent crusade ready to bomb the event and kill thousands of people who are worshiping inside. Instead he ends up at the front of the altar in tears of repentance and receives his adoption into the Kingdom of God. Later, he was physically rescued from the streets, taught to read and write, and was shown real love by a white man named Dr. Michael Cassidy.

Stephen is now the president of African Enterprise, an evangelical outreach ministry with offices in twenty countries all over the world. Funny that I would meet a man who lives in Malawi while in Hawaii. But meet him I did and that meeting had huge implications on my life, and maybe yours.

The morning I met Stephen, I was sitting at the very back of the conference room filled with 5,000 people when I actually heard God tell me to write this book. You might think I am completely nuts, but I am assuming that if you have made it to this chapter, you are still tracking with me. Yes, He told me to write this book. And I said, "No way!" Can

> After all that He has allowed me to go through and after saying "yes" to closing my business and "yes" to everything else, I said "no way" to God when He asked me to write.

you imagine? After all that He has allowed me to go through and after saying yes to closing my business and yes to everything else, I said no way to God when He asked me to write. God repeated himself to me, right there in the conference. He said in plain English, "It is time for you to write the book." I was thinking to myself, "You have got to be crazy if You think that I am going to open up my chest cavity and reveal my red and beating heart to the world by sharing my life with them. I can't handle that. Plus, I did a lot of stupid things I'm not proud of. I am not going to risk exposing myself to the world. No way."

Suddenly, a vision flashed through my brain of me sitting on Oprah's couch with the book in her hand and saying, "Don't you think it was really stupid to close your business?" Or worse, some magazine article written about the book saying, "Janine is obviously unstable and has no authority to be writing about Africa. She's just a business person and obviously not a very good one or she would still be doing it." Or worse yet—no one reading it! (Okay, so the Oprah thing may be a bit far fetched, but it did flash through my head . . . honestly.) So I said to God, as if He hadn't thought of this, "Okay God, who would want to read my story? Everybody has an amazing story. Who on earth would want to read mine?" And He answered. (I couldn't believe I was having a conversation with God, with 5,000 people sitting around me and no one else knew.)

He said, "Don't worry about who is going to read it, just write it as an act of obedience."

"NO! NO! NO! I am not going to do it. I can't. It will hurt too much. Haven't you put me through enough? Wasn't my business, my life, my family, and my heart enough for you, God? Don't make me do this. I can't. I won't." And I didn't tell a living soul, not even Ian because I knew he would be on my back about it.

So I left the meeting and went down to the area where the exhibition booths were, and there was Stephen Lungu. I had heard him give his testimony the day before and had read his book, *and* I was taking a team to Malawi later that year, so I wanted to introduce myself. His warm smile and big handshake made me feel like I had known him my whole life. I told him a bit about myself and Heart for Africa and about our upcoming trip to Malawi.

Now, I don't know how God did this, but somehow our short ten-minute conversation turned into Stephen telling me that I needed to be sharing my testimony. The story of having it all and then giving it all up to serve the poor in Africa was critical, and people in North America and Africa needed to hear it. He went on to say that people in Africa look at the American dream as their goal, and I had given up the dream to be obedient to my call. Great! Now God had total strangers on my case. No, I wasn't going to do it. (Many months later when I was in Malawi, I met with Stephen to thank him for being a catalyst for my writing to begin. He told me then that when we had met in Hawaii, the Lord had shown him a book beside my head, but he wasn't sure if he was to tell me that or not. I think I would have fainted if he had.)

So I continued developing a plan to move forward with Heart for Africa. The biggest question became where would we find the people to go on these trips and do the work? Ian and I were invited to San Diego for a fund-raising initiative hosted by one of our past trip volunteers named Caroline McGraw who also attends North Coast Calvary Chapel with her family. We gladly welcomed the trip as we missed our new friends there so much, and we thought we could discuss this very question with them. We had been included in the North Coast Calvary Chapel family, and we longed to go back and get fueled by them again.

The first morning we were there, we were fortunate enough to have a nice long breakfast with Mark and Jan Foreman. Oh, what a joy it was! Just like our first meeting, we laughed and cried. I felt like I had a full tank of gas at the end of our three hours; I certainly had a bladder full of coffee.

As we finished up, Jan invited me to speak the next morning at their women's conference themed: *If You Want to Walk on Water, You've Got to Get Out of the Boat*, which was based on a book written by John Ortberg. Jan was the opening speaker the next day for several hundred women, and she wanted to give me half her time. I couldn't believe it. She would talk about the premise behind the book and why we have to get out of the boat, and then I could be her case study. It was quite funny, but I did agree that I would be a good Exhibit A as I certainly had gotten out of the boat.

The next day with the ladies was great. Jan was great. When I had the opportunity to speak, I felt like I connected with the women like never before. I took Stephen Lungu's advice and gave my testimony—the whole thing. I was energized. I was on a roll. I was out of the boat and walking in faith!

But you know what I had done? I had gotten out of one boat and crawled into the one next to it. I wasn't walking in faith. I wasn't walking on water. I was hiding under the bow yelling "Row!" God had asked me to write a book and I was deliberately being disobedient. I must admit, closing ONYX seemed like an easier and more reasonable request to me than writing a book. I wanted anonymity. I wanted to serve and help quietly, out of the spotlight. I remember hearing the same Casting Crowns song again, as if for the first time. "The Voice of Truth" said:

> Oh what I would do to have
> The kind of faith it takes
> To climb out of this boat and then
> on to the crashing waves,
>
> To step out of my comfort zone
> Into the realm of the unknown where Jesus is
> And He's holding out His hand.
>
> But the waves are calling out my name
> And they laugh at me,
> Reminding me of all the times
> I've tried before and failed.
> The waves they keep on telling me
> Time and time again. "Boy, you never win!"
> "You never win!"
>
> Chorus:
> But the Voice of Truth tells me a different story.
> The Voice of Truth says, "Do not be afraid!"
> And the Voice of Truth says, "This is for My glory."
> Out of all the voices calling out to me,
> I will choose to listen and believe the Voice of Truth.

> God pursued me even through the music I listened to, and in the end I chose obedience.

God pursued me even through the music I listened to, and in the end I chose obedience. What I didn't realize was that this book is not about me, it is about Him and His plan for our lives. It is about God's heart for us, His children, and it is to show the great lengths that He will go to pursue us for His family, to adopt us as one of His own, and to give us His full inheritance.

In the summer of 2006 our family headed back to Africa for six weeks. This time we would be leading teams of people who were going to serve with Heart for Africa. It was a much different trip than the one only a short year before. This time our family started in Malawi, then headed down to meet the team in Swaziland, and then went back up to Malawi. Just before we left Canada, the Board of Directors decided that I really should be in full partnership with Ian at the head of Heart for Africa. Up until that point, I served alongside everyone else, but the Board felt a tug on their hearts that the mantle of Heart for Africa should be shared between Ian and me. After all (as I said to Ian), I'm the one who has the heart for Africa. I'm the African Queen! And so the Board officially invited me to take my place beside Ian. He would still be President (and take most of the bullets), but I would stand beside my husband and my best friend in serving God. I arrived in Africa for the first time as Dream for Africa became Heart for Africa, and I was a full partner in the ministry. Hmm. Why didn't that seem bigger to me? It was something I believed to be right. It was something I wanted, but something wasn't complete. I didn't know what, until the very end of our very last trip.

It had been a long six weeks of travel. And now that we were in charge, the burden was on us to ensure that everyone arrived safely and that our mission was accomplished in each area of service. Perfection is what we always aimed for at ONYX and perfection is what North American travelers hope for when they travel on these ten-day trips, but perfection is impossible when you are working in Africa. Absolutely impossible! The first rule that you must understand is that time is a North American thing, not an African thing. As Stephen Lungu once said, "In America you have watches, but no time. In Africa we have time, but no watches. Come to Africa and I will give you my time."

> "In America you have watches, but no time. In Africa we have time, but no watches. Come to Africa and I will give you my time."

I loved that saying, but I wish it wasn't quite so true. You can be as organized as a hive of bees and still arrive in a country to find out that all of the seedlings that you ordered six weeks prior have been sold to someone else. Not to worry, they can have more planted and ready in another six weeks, which would be exactly *five weeks too late for us to plant while we are here!* Now what would we plant? Or you can plan to send your entire group of fifty volunteers on a one-and-a-half-hour drive to a game reserve for a day to see African wildlife, only to find out that it is actually a five-hour drive each way (not including the blown tires that could not be fixed by putting on the non-existent spare!).

You do have to really be flexible to work in Africa. Each day was a new adventure for the Maxwell family, and we worked diligently to embrace it in that way. I will say that Ian's patience did wear thin when dealing with the Malawian currency of Kwatcha. There are approximately 140 Kwatcha to the US dollar. Imagine a cash-only country where you can't use your credit card to buy gasoline for your car (or multiple mini-vans that are driving your volunteers around). Now, consider that the largest bill in the currency is K500 equal to $3.57 U. S. Ian needed to carry around bails of cash in a dirt poor country to conduct daily business. It really was quite funny, or at least we chose to laugh.

Our final day of planting in Malawi was a warm one. The winter (our summer months) had ended only days before, and now the summer heat had been turned on like a furnace. From chills in the night air to a full-body sweat in the day, summer was upon us. Our dear friend and sister in the Lord, Theresa Malila, founder of *Somebody Cares* (the home care organization that we are working with in Malawi), insisted that I come with her to see her village that last morning. Chatimba village is where her father had been the chief for many years.

As her siblings had left the village and were dispersed throughout Africa, a new chief had to be carefully chosen to fulfill the role in the caring and serious way that Theresa's father had fulfilled it. Theresa herself had been made a chief in a large, formal festive ceremony that lasted for days. She is known as Chief Makhungula (which means Chief Mother, and that she is). As Theresa was not planning to move back to her village, they had also carefully chosen a man who lived there to be chief and to care for his people.

After our hour-long journey through either storms of orange dust that blocked our view beyond the front of the van, we arrived in Chatimba. The welcome was much more subdued than in any other village where I have been in Africa. The children were singing and happy, but there was a sense of shyness or uncertainty that I just couldn't put my finger on. How does one start to assess a quiet group of African children? When Theresa was asked why her village was responding to us so differently she laughed and said, "They have never seen white people before! They don't know what to think of you!" She laughed some more and then joined them in their dancing. Imagine that. They had never seen white people before. And why, we asked? Theresa explained that no one from Lilongwe would want to come way out here to meet these poor people, especially not white people. Why would anyone want to come here?

As we spoke, there was a commotion behind me. A big, orange leather chair appeared from the chief's house. It looked like it had first been a prop in the 1970s show Laugh In and had then had been donated to the village of Chatimba in deep, dark Africa. It was clearly a special piece of furniture and not used by just anyone. After it was put down on the dirt, several white doilies (same era) were carefully placed on the back, the seat and the armrests of this throne-like relic. I was pulled around to the side of the van where Theresa quickly wrapped an African cloth around my Canadian jeans to make a skirt (and make me presentable). Then she pushed me back to the crowd and told me to sit in the great, orange place of honor. I didn't know what was going on, but something was, to be sure. I saw Theresa speaking with the men in her family who still lived in the village and then to the head chief. They were in a deep conversation, and heads were nodding. The singing began, and suddenly everyone was looking at me in the orange chair with the doilies.

As I sat watching, the children began to come and gather around me. I later learned that the village had been decimated by the AIDS virus. They had buried forty-plus families and there were only thirty-eight couples left in the village. (They offered to take me to the graveyard to make a precise count, but I declined.). There were 500 children and 155 of them were orphans. When I asked who cared for them, they explained that the chief would "assign" a young teenager to live in the huts with the orphans and that teen would be held responsible for them as their guardian. I sat stunned. The numbers were real, we had heard them before over and over again, but I was sitting looking into the eyes of 155 children who had no parents and no hope for the future.

> If I looked carefully through the dirt on their faces and made eye contact, I could see glimpses of hope.

Suddenly, the singing began and a ceremony seemed to start. Everyone was looking at me and smiling. If I looked carefully through the dirt on their faces and made eye contact, I could see glimpses of hope. It was there. It wasn't completely gone, but their joy was. The singing started quietly as the children and some of the women gathered around me. They got on their knees as they sang and started to slowly crawl towards me as their voices got louder and louder. I didn't know what to think. I looked at Theresa, and she just grinned and joined in the singing and began clapping to the beat and dancing as only Theresa can. The chief stood proudly, and even he sang. But what was going on? I simply didn't know. But I knew it was significant. Then Theresa took a bunch of Kwatcha bills and started dancing around my chair and throwing money at me (I liked that part.) The children's smiles got bigger, their eyes began to light up, and they continued to crawl through the dirt on bare knees towards me. I looked to my right and couldn't believe my eyes. There was my own daughter, Chloe, on her knees with the other children, clapping and moving towards me.

That day in Malawi, I was made a chief. I am Chief Jambulani. I am a chief who was installed by the children. The song they sang said:

> *You are the mother of this community.*
> *We are your children.*
> *We are the children of the soil,*
> *We till the soil and water it.*

And then they looked at the chief and his elders who stood to my right and they sang:

> *We have seen the chief.*
> *She was alive when we installed her.*
> *If we find that she is dead tomorrow*
> *You will have to deal with us.*

And then they repeated:

> *You are the mother of this community.*
> *We are your children.*
> *We are the children of the soil,*
> *We till the soil and water it.*

It is unusual for a woman to be made a chief, but in the matriarchal tradition of Malawi, it is more common than in other African countries. Culturally, when a woman is made a chief, it is always the children who perform the installation. The warning they sang to the men comes from

> It was my chief's mantle—my true mantle for Heart for Africa. It had been made official by the very people who had the real authority to give it to me—the children of Africa.

a history of women who had been made chief later mysteriously dying in their sleep. So the children sang a strong warning to say that they see me alive, and I had better be alive in the morning. Comforting.

I didn't know what to do. I was truly speechless. I thought back to Bruce putting the mantle for Heart for Africa on Ian's shoulders. And then I thought about the Board of Directors verbally putting the mantle on me to share the ministry with Ian. But as these thoughts and images passed in slow motion through my head, I was aware of a piece of cloth being physically put around my shoulders. It was my chief's mantle—my true mantle for Heart for Africa. It had been made official by the very people who had the real authority to give it to me—the children of Africa. I was Chief Jambulani, mother to the community and to those children, "a new breed of mother" as was prophesied the year before in South Africa.

As I looked back at the children, I saw more women come and crawl toward me on their knees. They continued singing the song over and over again. Imagine us being there to plant Never Ending Gardens and the children singing, "We are the children of the soil. We till the soil and water it." And then out of nowhere came baskets of corn and ground nuts (peanuts) presented to me as gifts. My head was spinning. I truly didn't know what to do, so I sat quietly and tried to remember to breathe in and out. Breathe in and out.

It was August 2, 2006, when I saw the true heart of Africa, the heart that God sees every day, the heart that He is longing for us to see. It is the heart of the people, the men, women, and children who so desperately want to show us love and invite us into their world. They are not sitting with hands out saying, "What can you do for me?" They are saying, "Come and be a part of our family, our lives, and our community." Don't just come and visit for ten days. Come and join your heart with ours and together we will look toward a brighter tomorrow.

Heart for Africa has been redesigned to IGNITE a spark in people so that they want to go to Africa and serve on a short term trip. While there, we want you to EXPERIENCE the heart of Africa and all it has to offer. Then we want you to CONNECT with the people of Africa so that together we can help one another seek the very heart of God. Only then will there be salvation and transformation for all.

Come friend. Take my hand. Don't be afraid. We'll go together. One day we will witness this:

> When he finally arrives, blazing in beauty and all his angels with him, the Son of Man will take his place on his glorious throne. Then all the nations will be arranged before him and he will sort the people out, much as a shepherd sorts out sheep and goats, putting sheep to his right and goats to his left.

> Then the King will say to those on his right, "Enter, you who are blessed by my Father! Take what's coming to you

in this kingdom. It's been ready for you since the world's foundation. And here's why:

> I was hungry and you fed me,
> I was thirsty and you gave me a drink,
> I was homeless and you gave me a room,
> I was shivering and you gave me clothes,
> I was sick and you stopped to visit,
> I was in prison and you came to me."

Then those "sheep" are going to say, "Master, what are you talking about? When did we ever see you hungry and feed you, thirsty and give you a drink? And when did we ever see you sick or in prison and come to you?" Then the King will say, "I'm telling the solemn truth: Whenever you did one of these things to someone overlooked or ignored, that was me—you did it to me."

—Matthew 25:31–40 MSG

FINAL THOUGHTS FROM THE AUTHOR

On September 11, 2006, I sat and watched television's five-year anniversary memorials of the attacks on the twin towers. Each segment was specially designed to help us remember what had happened that tragic day. I spent hours watching photos that I had seen a million times before, both on TV and in my dreams. I spent hours hearing the stories of the survivors, the miracle stories of people being saved or spared. But what struck a cord with the innermost part of my heart was the voices of the children who had lost parents on that frightful day five years before. They spoke with great pride about the parent who had died, and often shared memories from before that day. But many of them had distanced themselves from the story they were telling. It was like something had changed and was fading away.

One young woman made it clear when she said, near the end of her speech (and I am paraphrasing since I didn't have pen and paper handy), "What makes me afraid now is that some days I can't remember what my dad looked like. I am forgetting his smell. I am forgetting the sound of his voice. I don't ever want to forget any of these things, but they are slipping away and I don't know what to do."

She broke my heart. I know how she feels. There are days that I sit at home in my new house in Atlanta and I somehow can't remember the smell of the slum—a smell that I never thought I would forget. And I ask if I will forget what Lillian's face looks like. Will I soon be unable to hear the wonderful singing and rhythm of the African music. And some days I don't even think once about those nine little children under the age of ten, living only one kilometer from where we lived in Swaziland. And then I get scared. What if I forget? The faces and the names and the voices and the smells of Africa are slipping away and I don't know what to do.

No one who has ever gone to Africa wants to forget. We all get on a plane to come home and we make commitments to ourselves, our family, and even our God to go back—to do something for the beautiful people who welcomed us into their lives without hesitation or expectation. But we all get caught in the distractions of our "real lives." We so want to help the people who hold our hearts, but their faces start to fade away as they are replaced with the faces of the people in our offices. The sight of their mud huts disappears as we frantically try to finish off the renovation on our own house or wash the dishes after a great dinner party. We thought the smiles on the little children could never be forgotten, but they too start to gray as we pick up our kids from piano lessons and drop them off at soccer. Before we even know it, we too are saying it's okay that they are hungry and thirsty and have no clothes or parents or education or safe home. And before you know it, it will all fade to black.

May I take a few more moments of your time and bring the picture back to color and focus? Thank you.

There are **30,000 children dying *every day*** in sub-Saharan Africa of hunger and/or malnutrition that means **2.9 million children** each and every year. Imagine, for a moment . . . they are actually dying of hunger. There are **fifteen million children** who have been orphaned by AIDS. In

2005 the prediction of the World Health Organization was that there would be forty-three million by the year 2010. They have now down-graded that prediction to be "only" eighteen million. Why is that? Is it because fewer people are dying? Or is it because the children are dying? It is the latter. When the parent dies, there is no one to feed the children? If there is no one there, the children will die and the forty-three million prediction drops to eighteen million, because **TWENTY-FIVE MILLION OF THEM WILL BE DEAD.** Twenty-five million children. Dead.

I ask you again. Is it okay with you that twenty-five million children will die because their parents died and left them orphans? Is it okay with you that one more child will die from hunger? Is it okay with you that today thousands of nine-year-old girls will have sex for bread? Is the picture becoming clearer in your mind?

Is your head starting to spin? But since our cognitive brains can't begin to process this, we throw up a defense mechanism and say, "Janine, I can't save twenty-five million children and neither can you. What do you want from me?" You are likely correct. You can not save twenty-five million children on your own and neither can I, but I ask you, what about Lillian? What about Kantwa? Weren't they worth saving? Didn't you rejoice when you read that they were safe and sound, protected from all that was happening to them? What about David who has now finished university and is out changing the world? Wasn't he worth the work and time and effort to save? What about _____? (Please insert your child's name in that blank, if you dare.) If you died and your child was hungry would it be okay with you that no one came to feed him or her? Would it be okay with you that people would have sex with him or her so your child could have a piece of bread?

You have read stories in this book about only a few of the children whom God gave me the privilege of witnessing rescued from certain death. But as I wrote each chapter, I realized that the reason he allowed me to see what I saw and hear what I heard and touch those I touched was so that I could tell *you* about it, first hand. My stories are not from other peoples memoirs, and my photos are not from the *National Geographic*. They were written and shot specifically for you to read and see. And today I stand as a witness before you to be the voice of truth about what is happening in Africa and to say that God is on the move.

Could you help one child? Not twenty-five million, but one? Jesus did. He died for "the one." It is hard for us to process that He would have gone to the cross just for me. Or just for you. If one is enough for Him, then it must be enough for us. Let's start with focusing on truly helping just one child or just one man or just one woman. Help to provide them with food and water and shelter and education. Help to provide them HOPE for a bright future by showing them that you do care and that it is not okay with you that they don't have those things that we take for granted. Do that and then you will see just how big God really is.

Am I saying that you have to close your successful business or quit your job or sell everything you have? You tell me. Has God put something in your heart that just won't fade away even though the faces and voices do? Do you hear a voice that is calling you to do something, but you just don't know what it is? Do you hear that voice and say, "But Janine, you don't understand. I have college tuition to pay. I own a successful financial services firm, I can't just leave. I am a mother of five; I can't just pack up and go." I am not asking you to do any of those things. But what I am asking you to do is listen to that one still small voice that *never* fades. Listen to what that voice is calling you to do.

> And I'll give them a heart to know me, God. They'll be my people and I'll be their God, for they'll have returned to me with all their heart.
>
> —Jeremiah 24:7

Have you heard His voice? I am here to invite you to step out of the boat in faith. The Father will never leave you nor forsake you. If it is He who has called you and asked you to serve, then I beg you to "Just Do It." I am living proof that when He calls, you will know it. And when you know it, you must act. He will direct your paths.

> We are faced with a decision that grows with urgency each passing day: Will we leave our small stories behind and venture forth to follow our Beloved into the Sacred Romance? The choice to become a pilgrim of the heart can happen any day and we can begin our journey from any place. We are here, the time is now, and the Romance is always unfolding. The choice before us not to make it happen.

> As G.K. Chesterton said, "An adventure is, by nature, a thing that comes to us. It is a thing that chooses us, not a thing we choose."

> Lucy wasn't looking for Narnia when she found it on the other side of the wardrobe; in a way, it found her. Abraham wasn't wandering about looking for the one true God; he showed up with an extraordinary invitation. But having had their encounters, both could have chosen otherwise. Lucy could have shut the wardrobe door and

never mentioned what had happened there. Abraham could have opted for life in Haran. The choice before us is a choice to enter in."

From *The Sacred Romance*
—Brent Curtis and John Elderidge*

Amen.

---

* Brent Curtis and John Eldridge, *The Sacred Romance* (Nashville: Thomas Nelson, 1997)

To learn more about the life of Charles Mulli please read:

Father to the Fatherless is the true story of a man whose life begins in desperate poverty, moves to riches, and finally servant-hood where he becomes a real-life demonstration of selfless love and sacrifice. His obedience challenges us to evaluate the cost of giving up all to God in the service of others.

To order visit **www.afcanada.com** or **www.BayRidgebooks.com** ISBN 1-897213-02-6

Visit **www.mullychildrensfamily.org** to find out more about Charles Mulli's amazing ministry to the orphaned, abandoned and abused children of Africa.

To learn more about the life of Stephen Lungu please read:

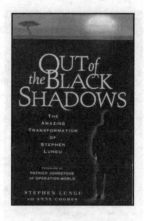

Stephen Lungu was the oldest son of a teenage mother, married off to a much older man by her parents, and living in a black township near Salisbury, Zimbabwe. When he was seven years old his mother ran away, leaving him on the street with his younger brother and sister. This story is one of miraculous transformation and will change the hearts of anyone who reads it.

To order visit **www.africanenterprise.org**—click on "Books".

If it's not okay with you either, please go to:
www.itsnotokaywithme.com
to see what you can do to make a difference in Africa.

Janine Maxwell currently lives in Atlanta, Georgia with her husband Ian and two children, Spencer and Chloe.

To book Janine Maxwell for a speaking engagement, please contact:

Heart for Africa
P.O. Box 573
Alpharetta, GA
30009
speaker@heartforafrica.org

For more information on **Heart for Africa** please go to:
www.heartforafrica.org

Hunger Orphans Poverty Education

Heart for Africa would like to sincerely thank the thousands of people who have traveled to Africa because it was "not okay" with them either. They heard the call and acted, working alongside us to touch, effect, and change the lives of thousands in Africa. We would also like to thank the individuals from the following churches, colleges and organizations for joining us as a vital part of the work of the body of Christ.

Baylor University—Waco, TX
Bethel Assembly of God—Tulare, CA
Biola University—La Mirada, CA
Calvary Church—Charlotte, NC
Canyon Hills Assembly of God—Bakersfield, CA
Cascade United Methodist Church—Atlanta, GA
Christ Memorial Reformed Church—Holland, MI
Clovis Hills Community Church—Clovis, CA
Crystal Cathedral—Garden Grove, CA
East 91st Street Christian Church—Indianapolis, IN
El Cajon Wesleyan Church—El Cajon, CA
Faith Chapel—Spring Valley, CA
First Presbyterian Church of Honolulu—Kaneohe, HI
Flood Church—San Diego, CA
Great Hills Baptist Church—Austin, TX
Hope College—Holland, MI
Moody Bible Institute—Chicago, IL
Mount Pisgah United Methodist Church—Alpharetta, GA
Mountaintop Community Church—Birmingham, AL
North Coast Calvary Chapel—Carlsbad, CA
North Point Community Church—Alpharetta, GA
Nuuanu Baptist Church—Honolulu, HI
Oak Cliff Bible Fellowship—Dallas, TX
Peoples Church—Fresno, CA
Reedley Mennonite Brethren Church—Reedley, CA
Shadow Mountain Community Church—El Cajon, CA
Trinity Christian College—Palos Heights, IL
Unionville Alliance Church—Unionville, ON Canada

To order additional copies of this title call:
1-877-421-READ (7323)
or please visit our web site at
www.winepressbooks.com

If you enjoyed this quality custom published book,
drop by our web site for more books and information.

www.winepressgroup.com
"Your partner in custom publishing."